LEVEL F • GRADE 1

Integrated Performance Assessment

Teacher's Manual with Assessment Forms

Dr. Roger Farr, Director,
Center for Reading and Language Studies at Indiana University

HB Assessment Group,
a Professional Assessment Company

HOLT, RINEHART AND WINSTON
Harcourt Brace & Company
Austin • New York • Orlando • Atlanta • San Francisco • Boston • Dallas • Toronto • London

STAFF CREDITS

Project Director: Kathleen Daniel
Executive Editor: Mescal K. Evler
Managing Editor: Robert R. Hoyt
Project Editors: Richard Blake, Scott Hall, Amy Strong
Editorial Staff: Julie Barnett, Joel Bourgeois, Roger Boylan, Jeffrey T. Holt, Katherine E. Hoyt, Constance D. Israel, Carrie Laing Pickett, Atietie O. Tonwe, Michael Webb
Editorial Support Staff: Ruth A. Hooker, Roni Franki, Kelly Keeley, Margaret Sanchez, Pat Stover
Editorial Permissions: Ann Farrar
Sr. Art Director: Pun Nio
Cover Design: Bob Bretz
Interior Design: Janet Brooks, Alicia Sullivan
Packaging Design: Joe Melomo
Production Coordinator: Rosa Mayo Degollado
Manufacturing Coordinator: Michael Roche

ABOUT THE AUTHOR

Dr. Roger Farr is currently Chancellor's Professor of Education and Director of the Center for Reading and Language Studies at Indiana University. He is a past president of the International Reading Association and the author of both traditional norm-referenced tests and performance assessments. Dr. Farr has taught at both elementary and high school levels in New York State and has served as a school district reading consultant.

The International Reading Association presented Dr. Farr the William S. Gray award for outstanding lifetime contributions to the teaching of reading in 1984. He was elected to the IRA Reading Hall of Fame in 1986 and was selected by the IRA as the Outstanding Teacher Educator in Reading in 1988.

ASSESSMENT DESIGN

Gene Jongsma, David Markson and Tami Steelman of HB Assessment Group

EXCERPTED MATERIALS

The following selection was excerpted from its original source for instructional purposes:
From *Hunger of Memory* by Richard Rodriguez (page 76)

Printed in the United States of America

ISBN 0-03-095104-6

345 022 00 99 98

CONTENTS

TO THE TEACHER
USING *INTEGRATED PERFORMANCE ASSESSMENT* WITH READING AND WRITING PROGRAMS

The design of the *Integrated Performance Assessment* program allows you to adapt it for use in a wide variety of instructional settings. Each assessment consists of a Reading section and a Writing section. The Reading section provides one or two authentic literary selections and a series of open-ended questions that are scored holistically. The Writing section provides prewriting activities and a prompt that elicits a specific form of writing, and culminates in holistic scores for both Rhetorical Effectiveness and Conventions. The Reading and Writing sections may be administered either together or independently.

The chart on the following page suggests where you might most effectively use *Integrated Performance Assessment* in each of the following textbooks.

ELEMENTS OF LITERATURE

Integrated Performance Assessment Level F — Grade 11 correlates with the instructional program of *Elements of Literature, Fifth Course.* Each assessment uses a reading selection that is thematically linked to its respective collection in the literature textbook. In addition, the selection represents a reading genre (e.g., poem, short story, folktale) that the students experience in those collections. Similarly, the writing section of the assessment evaluates the writing forms that are taught in the correlating collections.

ADVENTURES IN LITERATURE

Integrated Performance Assessment Level F — Grade 11 may be readily adapted for use with *Adventures in American Literature.* In some instances the writing form may appear in a different *Adventures* unit than the reading genre.

ELEMENTS OF WRITING

Integrated Performance Assessment Level F — Grade 11 may also be used for holistic evaluation of writing forms taught in *Elements of Writing, Fifth Course.*

OTHER PROGRAMS

Integrated Performance Assessment Level F — Grade 11 is easily adapted to most reading and writing programs. If you are teaching an integrated program, you may wish to use both sections of each assessment. Or, you may use just the section appropriate to your curriculum. If you are using the Reading assessment with a program not listed on the following chart, you should check for duplication of the reading assignment in your classroom materials. In case a duplication occurs, you may want to administer the Reading assessment in this manual before teaching the selection.

Correlation Chart: Integrated Performance Assessment, Level F—Grade 11

ASSESSMENT	ELEMENTS OF LITERATURE, FIFTH COURSE	ADVENTURES IN AMERICAN LITERATURE	ELEMENTS OF WRITING, FIFTH COURSE	READING PASSAGE (GENRE)	WRITING FORM (TASK)
1	Beginnings: 1450–1800	Unit 1 (Reading) Unit 4 (Writing)	Chapter 4 (Writing only)	"The Author to Her Book" by Anne Bradstreet (Poem)	Observational Essay (Descriptive) • Write an article for the local newspaper about someone who is creative.
2	The American Renaissance: A Literary Coming of Age: 1830–1860	Unit 3 (Reading) Unit 2 (Writing)	Chapter 8 (Writing only)	"The Masque of the Red Death" by Edgar Allan Poe (Short Story)	Persuasive Essay (Persuasive) • Write a letter to the editor of the school newspaper taking a position on a controversial issue.
3	The Rise of Realism: The Civil War and Postwar Period: 1860–1915	Unit 7 (Reading) Unit 3 (Writing)	Chapter 10 (Writing only)	"How It Feels to Be Colored Me" by Zora Neale Hurston (Autobiographical Essay)	Interpretation (Expository) • Write an essay for the English teacher that interprets images used by the author.
4	American Drama	Unit 7 (Reading) Unit 5 (Writing)	Chapter 6 (Writing only)	From *Hunger of Memory* by Richard Rodriguez (Autobiographical Essay, excerpt)	Evaluation (Persuasive) • Write an essay for the English teacher that evaluates and compares the author's criteria for choosing books with your own.

INTEGRATED PERFORMANCE ASSESSMENT
HOLISTIC SCORING WORKSHOP

The *Holistic Scoring Workshop* is an easy-to-use tutorial program that introduces teachers to holistic scoring and provides opportunities to practice scoring actual student papers. This unique software program is directly correlated with the *Integrated Performance Assessment Teacher's Manual with Assessment Forms.* Call 1-800-225-5425 for prices. The program consists of two main sections shown in the Main Menu below.

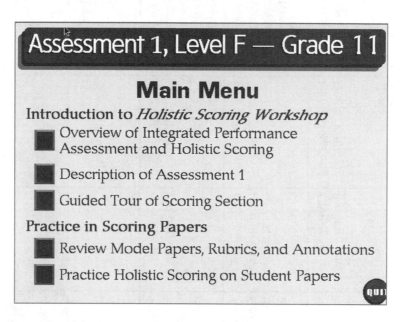

• **Overview of Integrated Performance Assessment and Holistic Scoring** This section of the program introduces teachers to the basic principles of integrated performance assessment and its key feature, holistic scoring. The overview explains the rationale underlying the development of this form of assessment and offers a general introduction to holistic scoring.

• **Description of Assessment** This section previews the content of the specific assessment. It tells how to prepare for scoring reading and writing responses to that assessment and shows how to apply the rubrics to the assessment.

• **Guided Tour of Scoring Section** This section provides an annotated preview of the scoring training program.

• **Review Model Papers, Rubrics, and Annotations** This section allows teachers to try out the training program's features before entering an actual practice scoring session. In this section teachers can explore the rubrics for reading, rhetorical effectiveness, and conventions; view model student papers that illustrate high, medium, and low levels of performance; and read annota-

tions that analyze the student papers and explain the scores that were assigned.

• **Practice Holistic Scoring on Student Papers** In this section teachers can apply what they have learned. Ten practice papers—five in reading and five in writing—are provided for each assessment. As teachers read and analyze the practice papers, they can access the rubrics, model papers, and annotations to clarify their scoring judgments. After scoring a paper, they can compare their evaluation to those of experienced scorers and read an analysis of the paper they have scored. A cumulative summary table updates and displays the percentage of agreement between the teacher's evaluation and that of an experienced scorer.

The *Holistic Scoring Workshop* is a valuable supplement to the *Integrated Performance Assessment Teacher's Manual with Assessment Forms.* The program is an ideal introduction and training tool for teachers who have little experience with holistic scoring. For more experienced teachers who may wish to refresh their holistic scoring skills, the program serves as a helpful review.

INTEGRATED
PERFORMANCE
ASSESSMENT

Introduction to Integrated Performance Assessment

The integrated performance assessments presented in this manual offer a unique and meaningful approach to gauging student performance. These new assessments help bridge the gap between instruction and assessment by modeling good instruction. Thus, assessment becomes a more integral part of the instructional program.

Rationale for Integrated Performance Assessment

Integrated performance assessment reflects three major trends in English education. First, many instructional programs now emphasize an integrated approach to language arts instruction—one in which reading, writing, listening, and speaking are taught in combination, not as separate subjects. Second, greater emphasis is placed on reading a variety of types of literature, some of which represent a multicultural perspective. Third, students are taught to view writing as a process in which ideas are generated, organized, revised, refined, and eventually published or shared.

The integrated performance assessments in this program were developed to
- approximate the reading, writing, speaking, and listening activities that students will encounter in most language arts programs as well as in daily life
- include a variety of reading and writing genres
- encourage students to write for different purposes and for different audiences

The following key principles guided the development of the integrated performance assessments.

➤ *Students should have opportunities to respond to a variety of types of literature.*
In the typical literature classroom students are exposed to a variety of reading materi-

als—fiction and nonfiction, poetry, plays, and many other types. The integrated performance assessments reflect this literary diversity. They capture the richness and variety in children's literature and in young adult literature.

➤ *Students should have opportunities to write for different purposes and in different modes.*
The integrated performance assessments tap a variety of writing purposes and writing modes. The writing tasks were created to reflect the types of writing many students do in the classroom as well as the types of writing found in many state and district assessments. Each assessment presents a unique writing task.

➤ *Periodically teachers should have students respond to a "standard" reading and writing task.*
An effective English education program gives students choices—both in what they read and in what they write. However, from time to time it is also useful, for purposes of evaluation, to have all students respond to the same task, or assessment. The four assessments in this manual may be used for quarterly assessment or may be administered whenever the teacher desires to check performance.

Features of these Integrated Performance Assessments

➤ *They model good instruction.*
The assessments are like "mini-lessons." By eliciting reading responses and modeling the writing process they provide instructional value.

➤ *They use authentic literature.*
Each assessment is based on a selected piece of published literature with a different theme for each selection. Some of the assessments use complete short stories and poems; others use excerpts from longer works such as novels and plays.

Many of the reading selections were written by well-known authors.

➤ *They encourage process writing.*
The assessments guide students through the process of generating and organizing their ideas. Students are given an opportunity to revise their initial drafts and create published works.

➤ *They permit collaboration.*
An optional collaborative activity is included in the writing section of the integrated performance assessments. If the

teacher desires, students can share their writing plans with classmates to gather reactions and suggestions for improving their writing.

➤ *They are diagnostic.*
By collecting students' prewriting notes and preliminary drafts, teachers can gain valuable insights into the reading, writing, and thinking strategies that students are using. The optional Speaking/Listening Observational Checklist and Reading/ Writing Observational Checklist can also identify strengths and weaknesses in students.

➤ *They are flexible.*
No strict time limits are imposed, and students are encouraged to proceed at their own rate within the class time allocated for the assessment.

➤ *They are scored holistically.*
Students' responses to the reading selection are scored holistically. Likewise, responses to the writing prompt are scored holistically for rhetorical effectiveness and conventions. Thus, the integrated performance assessments offer a comprehensive view of student performance.

AN OVERVIEW OF THE INTEGRATED PERFORMANCE ASSESSMENTS FOR LEVEL F—GRADE 11

Four assessments have been developed for use at Level F—Grade 11. The following table summarizes the characteristics of each of these assessments.

Integrated Performance Assessments for Level F—Grade 11

ASSESSMENT FORM	READING PASSAGE (GENRE)	WRITING FORM (TASK)
1	"The Author to Her Book" by Anne Bradstreet (Poem)	Observational Essay (Descriptive) • Write an article for the local newspaper about someone who is creative.
2	"The Masque of the Red Death" by Edgar Allan Poe (Short Story)	Persuasive Essay (Persuasive) • Write a letter to the editor of the school newspaper taking a position on a controversial issue.
3	"How It Feels to Be Colored Me" by Zora Neale Hurston (Autobiographical Essay)	Interpretation (Expository) • Write an essay for the English teacher that interprets images used by the author.
4	From *Hunger of Memory* by Richard Rodriguez (Autobiographical Essay, excerpt)	Evaluation (Persuasive) • Write an essay for the English teacher that evaluates and compares the author's criteria for choosing books with your own.

DEVELOPMENT OF INTEGRATED PERFORMANCE ASSESSMENT

The integrated performance assessments in this program were developed in collaboration with Dr. Roger Farr and the Center for Reading and Language Studies at Indiana University. This Center was chosen because of its wide range of experience in developing and scoring performance tasks. Development of the assessments took place over an extended period and involved several stages. Each major stage in that developmental process is briefly described below.

1. **Identify eligible reading genre and themes and eligible writing forms.** In order to create assessments that actually evaluate what is taught in most literature programs, it was necessary to identify the specific reading themes and genre and the specific writing forms and tasks that could be used at each grade level.

2. **Select an appropriate format and scoring system.** A review was made of performance assessments cited in the professional literature, as well as those used in state testing programs. Comparisons were made among the available models, and desirable features were identified. Holistic scoring was chosen as the primary method of scoring.

3. **Identify potential literature selections to use in the assessments.** Several factors influenced the selection of reading passages. First, it was important to include pieces that represented a multicultural perspective. Second, the passages had to be interesting and engaging to students. And third, they had to be of appropriate difficulty and length.

4. **Identify field-test sites.** Each assessment was field tested and evaluated with students before it was selected for publication. The field-test sites represented a variety of geographic locations and district sizes and involved diverse student populations. A list of field-test sites can be found in the Appendix.

5. **Conduct field tests of the assessments.** Field tests were conducted in the fall of 1994 and the spring of 1995 in a number of school districts across the United States. Field-test versions of the assessments were distributed to participating teachers. Teachers administered the assessments following directions very similar to those included in this manual. After completing the assessments, teachers and students evaluated them through survey questionnaires. The questionnaires addressed topics such as the appropriateness of the reading selections, student interest in the selections, the appropriateness of the writing task, student interest in the writing task, and the clarity of the questions and directions.

6. **Analyze the field test results.** For analysis, all student papers and questionnaires were returned to the Center for Reading and Language Studies. Teams of experienced readers scored the student responses to each prompt and reviewed the questionnaire results. Based on the data that were collected, judgments were made as to which prompts were working well and were engaging to students. At this point, some assessments were rejected and replaced with new ones or modified and sent out for additional field testing; others were accepted as suitable.

7. **Select the model or benchmark papers.** After the assessments to be published were selected, the total pool of student papers for each one was reviewed by a panel of judges who selected model papers to illustrate various score points. Annotations were then written for each model paper explaining and justifying the score it was given. The model papers and annotations are in the Appendix of this manual.

The entire developmental process was comprehensive and thorough. It gave the publisher a firsthand look at how students and teachers reacted to integrated performance assessment, and an opportunity to drop or correct assessments that were not working as expected.

EVIDENCE OF VALIDITY AND RELIABILITY

A test or assessment that is not valid and reliable is of little value. It is important for an assessment to measure what it claims to measure, and for it to do so consistently.

➤ *Validity*
The validity of an assessment is judged relative to the purpose for which it will be used. To answer the question, "Is this test valid?", one must first ask "for what purpose?" For example, a test that assesses knowledge of the alphabet could be extremely valid in predicting success in early reading, but not valid in predicting success in graduate school. The integrated performance assessments presented in this work were designed for the purpose of evaluating a student's ability to comprehend and interpret literature, and to write effectively. Therefore, they must be evaluated in light of these purposes.

As part of the field tests, teachers and students independently judged the validity of the assessment they took part in. They rated the quality of the assessment in terms of how well it measures reading ability, writing ability, thinking ability, and group communication.

The results show that teachers and students viewed the integrated performance assessments as valid measures of reading, writing, thinking, and communicating. The overwhelming majority of teachers and students thought the assessments measured reading, writing, and thinking "very well" or "well." It is interesting to note that students perceived these assessments as valid measures as often as teachers did.

➤ *Reliability*

Reliability refers to consistency in scoring. If two readers scored the same paper independently, would they assign it the same score? Data collected during the scoring process showed that readers were in exact agreement 60 to 70 percent of the time; differed by one score point 25 to 35 percent of the time; and differed by two or more points 5 percent of the time or less. These results applied to all three scales that are used in the integrated performance assessments. These results are consistent with those reported in the research literature for similar types of holistic scoring.

ADMINISTERING INTEGRATED PERFORMANCE ASSESSMENT

The integrated performance assessments in this manual may represent a new type of testing for some teachers. Unlike many traditional forms of testing, integrated performance assessment does not use standardized directions for administering and does not impose specific time limits on students. Teachers should feel free to alter the directions for administering the assessment to suit their students as well as local conditions.

GENERAL GUIDELINES

1. **Be interactive.** The assessments are a dynamic form of measurement. That means that you can, and should, interact with students while they are completing the activity. The basic rule of thumb is "test the way you teach."

2. **Be encouraging.** Your role in administering the assessments should be that of a coach. You should motivate, guide, prod, and encourage students to produce their best work.

3. **Be supportive.** You may assist students who need help. The amount of assistance you provide can range from very little to quite a bit, depending on the needs and abilities of your students. If students are unfamiliar with this type of activity, you may need to offer more guidance on the first few assessments that students complete. However, as students become more familiar with the process, you should encourage greater independence.

4. **Be clear.** The directions for administering the assessments are not standardized. If necessary, you should paraphrase the directions for students. The goal is to communicate clearly to students the nature of the task and what they are to do.

5. **Be flexible.** Not all students have to proceed through the assessment at the same rate and in the same manner. On the Writing section, for example, some students may be ready to write their first drafts while others are still planning their writing.

6. **Be reflective.** Whenever possible, encourage students to engage in self-evaluation. The Writing section of each assessment contains a set of questions intended to encourage students to judge their own work. Peer conferences may also be used to foster self-evaluation.

7. **Be fair.** Allow students adequate time to do their best work. It would be unfair to set high expectations for students and then not give them enough time to fulfill those expectations.

OPTIONS FOR ADMINISTERING INTEGRATED PERFORMANCE ASSESSMENT

These integrated performance assessments have been designed to offer teachers maximum flexibility in time and method of administration. Each assessment is composed of two main sections — a Reading section and a Writing section. The following table displays the components of an integrated performance assessment.

INTEGRATED PERFORMANCE ASSESSMENT	
Reading Section	**Writing Section**
Getting Ready to Read Time to Read Responding to the Selection	Getting Ready to Write Sharing Your Plans with Others (Optional) Thinking About Reactions Time to Write

There are basically three options for administering the assessments. The following table summarizes the features of each option.

OPTION	PURPOSE	TIME NEEDED
Administer the Reading section only	To assess a student's ability to interpret and critically evaluate a piece of literature	Approximately one class period
Administer the Writing section only	To assess a student's ability to use a specific writing form and write effectively	Approximately one class period
Administer both the Reading section and the Writing section	To gain a comprehensive view of a student's reading and writing skills	Two to three class periods

Because all of the integrated performance assessments are structured in the same way, the following directions can be used for any of them.

Administering the Reading Section (1 class period)

STEP 1: Become familiar with the reading selection and the prompts that follow it.
STEP 2: Read the directions for the Reading section found in the student booklet aloud to the class. Paraphrase the directions if necessary and answer any questions.
STEP 3: Have students read the passage independently and respond to the prompts that follow the passage.

Administering the Writing Section (1 or 2 class periods)

STEP 1: Read the "Getting Ready to Write" part of the Writing section aloud to the class to explain the writing task.
STEP 2: Have students do their initial planning independently.
STEP 3: (Optional) Allow students to share their writing plans with classmates.
STEP 4: Encourage students to think about reactions they may have received, revise their prewriting plans, and begin drafting.
STEP 5: Decide if this is a "first-draft" assessment or a polished piece. If it is a first-draft assessment, establish a time limit (e.g., 45 minutes) and inform students when their drafts will be due. If a polished piece is the goal, extend the time by an additional session or class period, permitting students more time to revise and edit their work.

USING COLLABORATION WHEN ADMINISTERING ASSESSMENTS

Collaboration has become an important part of English language arts instruction for many teachers. Research has shown, for example, that our interpretations are often shaped and influenced by the social communities that we are a part of. Likewise, peer review and other forms of collaboration have become standard parts of process writing instruction.

If collaboration is an important part of the instructional program, it should be incorporated into the assessments as well. Listed below are some suggestions as to when discussion groups could be used. The teacher could select the most appropriate point at which to use collaboration based on her or his instructional goals:
• after reading the selection
• after answering the reading response items
• after formulating some initial writing plans
• after completing a first draft

The teacher can gather additional insights about students' communication skills by systematically observing them while they work on an integrated performance assessment.

The optional **Reading/Writing Observational Checklist** is designed to be used while the students are working on an integrated performance assessment. The checklist should be used to observe an individual student or small group of students, not an entire class. Therefore, before administering an assessment, the teacher should decide which student(s) to observe. For example, the teacher may target a student who has been exhibiting difficulty in class or perhaps a small group of students who have been receiving supplemental instruction.

The **Reading/Writing Observational Checklist** is composed of two parts. **Part 1: Observing the Reading Process** lists strategies that effective readers use.

Part 2: Observing the Writing Process focuses on important aspects of the writing process, such as planning, revising, and self-evaluating. A copying master of the checklist is in the Appendix.

To use the checklist, write across the bottom of the form the names of the students you wish to observe. As students read the passage individually, walk around the classroom and monitor their efforts. By talking with students about their reading and observing their reactions, you can make inferences about the strategies they are using. Use the marking key on the form to record how consistently they use the effective reading strategies.

You may wish to use the back of the checklist to note whether the students requested assistance while reading and what kind of assistance they needed. You may also want to record other relevant observations that do not fit the categories in the checklist in this area.

The best time to use **Part 2** of the checklist **(Observing the Writing Process)** is while students are working on the Writing section of an integrated performance assessment. Circulate around the room, and observe what the students are doing. Use the marking key to record which strategies they are using and how consistently they use them.

The **Reading/Writing Observational Checklist** can be valuable in planning instruction. After you have recorded your observations, look for patterns. Are there particular strategies that students are not using? If so, these can be addressed in teacher-student conferences or in future lessons.

The optional **Speaking/Listening Observational Checklist** is also intended to be used to record observations of an individual student or a small group of students while they are working on an integrated performance assessment. It is designed to focus on positive speaking and listening behaviors. A copying master of this checklist can be found in the Appendix.

Decide in advance which students you want to observe. Then write their names in the boxes at the bottom of the checklist. You may observe speaking and listening at many points during the integrated performance assessment, depending on how much collaboration you have built into the assessment. For example, the checklist could be used to observe small group discussions following the reading phase or during the prewriting phase.

The information you gather on the **Speaking/Listening Observational Checklist** should be helpful in planning instruction. It may suggest, for example, which students need to be more involved in group discussions and which students need to focus on listening to the comments of others.

PROVIDING FOR STUDENTS WITH SPECIAL NEEDS

Many school districts are faced with the challenge of adapting instruction and assessment to meet the needs of special learners. These may be students for whom English is a second language, as well as students who are physically, emotionally, or intellectually challenged. Because the integrated performance assessments are not standardized, the procedures for administering them can be adjusted to meet the needs of special learners.

You may help students who have difficulty reading the selections independently by
- providing audiotapes of the reading selections and reading along with the narration
- pairing a less proficient reader with a more proficient reader in a buddy system and allowing the more able student to provide assistance when needed
- providing assistance (e.g., pronouncing difficult words, explaining unfamiliar concepts) upon request

- permitting students to take the reading selection home to have a parent, friend, or sibling read it to them

Teachers may help students who have difficulty responding to the writing assessments by
- encouraging them to discuss their prewriting ideas with a partner before actually starting to write
- permitting them to create an audiotape of their ideas in lieu of a written response
- allowing them to do their initial planning, drafting, revising, and editing on a computer
- giving them extra time to do their planning and drafting

Keep in mind that the more the performance assessments are modified the less reliable they may be as measures of students' *independent* reading and writing abilities.

HOLISTIC SCORING OF
INTEGRATED PERFORMANCE ASSESSMENT

Each integrated performance assessment yields three scores—one for reading, and two for writing.

READING ✔	**WRITING: Rhetorical Effectiveness** ✔ **Conventions** ✔

The scores, which can range from a low of 1 to a high of 6, are determined by a process of holistic scoring. That is, a student's work is gauged by the criteria specified in the scoring rubrics. Model papers are provided in the Appendix to illustrate and define the criteria embodied in the rubrics.

GENERAL GUIDELINES FOR HOLISTIC SCORING

Holistic scoring has been used for many years to evaluate writing samples. Many state writing assessments, for example, employ some form of holistic scoring. In holistic scoring, the reader takes several features into consideration—weighing and balancing strengths in one feature against weaknesses in others—to arrive at a single, overall score. Holistic scoring is generally faster to do than analytic scoring, which requires separate judgments about each of several factors or features.

SCORING THE READING SECTION

In the **Reading** section of integrated performance assessment, a student reads an authentic selection, or two shorter selections, and responds to a series of five to eight open-ended questions. The questions are not scored individually. Rather, the student's responses to all the questions are considered, and a single reading score is given for the entire section.

The questions in the Reading section have been designed to assess a student's ability to construct a personal interpretation of a text. More specifically, the questions assess four levels of response from the student.

First thoughts. This refers to a reader's initial reaction to what was read. It draws on the reader's immediate images, feelings, opinions, and memories of the text. It typically involves a consideration of the text as a whole rather than of its specific parts.

Shaping interpretations. Here the reader extends his or her first thoughts, often making links across different parts of the text to arrive at a deeper, more thoughtful understanding. The reader attempts to construct a personal interpretation of the text through activities such as identifying the theme, making analogies, speculating on the motives of characters, and exploring alternative interpretations. When shaping interpretations, the reader may return to the text to confirm or revise judgments and/or seek additional evidence. As part of this process the reader may exhibit metacognitive awareness of his or her ability to process the text.

Connecting with the text. This assessment examines the reader's ability to make associations between the text and life outside of the text. Connections may be made between the text and other readings, or between the text and other media such as plays, movies, or television programs. In making connections, the reader may apply his or her understanding of human nature to the text; may form analogies between the world of the text and his or her personal world; and may make associations between a character's life and his or her own situation. In essence, the reader strives to connect the text to personal experience.

Challenging the text. The reader must step outside of the text to challenge the text, and/or to make critical judgments of quality about parts of the text or the text as a whole. For example, the reader may make judgments of the literary quality of the text; contrast types of writing styles or genres; analyze the use of specific literary features; agree or disagree with the author's point of view; speculate on how the author might have treated the subject differently; or show aesthetic appreciation of the text.

SCORING RUBRIC FOR READING

The **General Scoring Rubric for Reading** is shown on the next several pages. This version of the rubric may be considered the unabridged version in that it provides a rather extensive description of each score point. Note that four paragraphs are included for each score point. The paragraphs correspond to the four levels of response to reading explained previously.

Because some teachers might find the General Scoring Rubric too extensive and perhaps too complex to use as a reference during actual scoring, an **Abbreviated Scoring Rubric for Reading** can be found in the **Appendix**. This abridged version summarizes the key criteria contained in the complete rubric.

GENERAL SCORING RUBRIC FOR READING
USED FOR ALL ASSESSMENT FORMS

SCORE 1 MINIMAL READING PERFORMANCE

The student displays minimal understanding or serious misunderstanding of the text. Responses suggest that the student is processing the text at the word or sentence level. Difficult sections of the text cause frustration and may result in efforts to abandon the text (e.g., "This is boring!" "I hate this story!" "This story doesn't make sense").

The student displays no reflective thinking either about the text or his or her ability to process it. Any attempt to make meaning is fragmented and focuses on parts of the text rather than the coherent whole. The student makes no attempt to generalize beyond the text, and responses show no evidence of meaningful engagement with the text. There is no evidence of meaningful emotional or intellectual engagement with the text.

The student displays no meaningful association between the text and other texts, other media, and/or personal experience, and is unable to recognize any relevance the text has to understanding human nature. The student displays no ability to make meaningful, critical judgments about the text, or to show aesthetic appreciation. Any evaluative comments or challenges to the author or text tend to be emotional rather than rational.

SCORE 2 LIMITED READING PERFORMANCE

The student displays a limited or superficial understanding of the text. The responses are likely to focus on selected segments of the text rather than on the text as a whole. Text difficulties (e.g., ambiguities, contradictions) are disruptive to the reader.

The student displays little, if any, reflective thinking about the text or his or her ability to process it. Any attempt to express significant understanding of the text (e.g., theme, point of view) is simplistic and superficial. The student finds it difficult to generalize beyond the text and is more likely to settle for a literal understanding. Alternative interpretations are seldom explored. The student shows little emotional or intellectual engagement with the text.

The student displays difficulty in making associations between the text and other texts, other media, and/or personal experience. Associations that are made are superficial and lack depth of understanding. The student is likely to engage in autobiographical digressions that bear little relevance to the text and shows little, if any, awareness of how the text may contribute to one's understanding of human nature.

The student displays limited ability to evaluate the text critically and shows little, if any, aesthetic appreciation of the text. Judgments of quality tend to be emotional and/or unsupported. The student tends to accept the text without questioning ideas, and discounts or ignores the text when it violates personal experience.

SCORE 3   LITERAL READING PERFORMANCE

The student displays a plausible but simplistic understanding of the text. For the most part, the student interprets the text literally. When difficulties are encountered in the text (e.g., ambiguities, contradictions), they tend to be ignored.

The student displays little reflective thinking about the text or about his or her ability to process it. Attempts to express an understanding of the text as a whole are fairly predictable and lack original insights. The student demonstrates some engagement with the text, but this connection may be more emotional than intellectual. The student shows little willingness to revise or reshape his or her interpretation based on new evidence or new understanding.

The student may make associations between the text and other texts, other media, and/or personal experience, but the associations tend to lack depth or to be unsupported. The student is not likely to challenge the author or text, and generally accepts his or her first interpretation without exploring alternative interpretations. The student displays little awareness of how the text may contribute to an understanding of human nature.

The student displays limited ability to evaluate the text critically, and the evaluations tend not to be well supported. There is little evidence of challenging the text, questioning the author, engaging in reflective reading, or showing aesthetic appreciation.

SCORE 4   THOUGHTFUL READING PERFORMANCE

The student displays a thoughtful understanding of the whole text. Responses show evidence of using cues within the text to fill in gaps, create meaning, and differentiate between literal and figurative meanings. The student may show some ability to deal effectively with text difficulties (e.g., ambiguities, contradictions).

The student displays some reflective thinking about the text but does not exhibit the deeper interpretations of more discerning readers. The student attempts to express an understanding of the text as a whole and constructs a personal interpretation that goes beyond a literal understanding, but is reluctant to explore alternative interpretations of the text. There is some evidence of emotional and intellectual engagement with the text.

The student makes some associations between the text and other texts, other media, and/or personal experience, but the associations tend to be routine and predictable. The student displays evidence of using his or her understanding of human nature to interpret the text and displays some awareness of how the text contributes to an understanding of human nature.

The student displays some ability to evaluate the text critically, but the evaluations tend to lack original insights. There may be some evidence of questioning the author, challenging the text, engaging in reflective reading, or showing aesthetic appreciation.

SCORE 5   DISCERNING READING PERFORMANCE

The student displays a thoughtful and perceptive understanding of the whole text, but the interpretation lacks the insights of exemplary readers. Responses show evidence of high-order processing. The student deals effectively with text difficulties (e.g., ambiguities, contradictions).

The student displays reflective thinking about the text but may lack the deeper interpretations exhibited by superior readers. There is evidence of emotional and intellectual engagement with the text and a willingness to explore alternative interpretations and search for a deeper understanding. The student may exhibit an awareness of his or her ability to process the text.

The student displays associations between the text and other texts, other media, and/or personal experience, and usually supports those judgments with evidence, but the associations may not be as thoughtful as those of exemplary readers. The student uses personal knowledge to interpret the text and may arrive at a new or clarified understanding of human nature.

The student displays some sensitivity to linguistic, cultural, and psychological features of the text; makes critical evaluations of the text; and usually supports those evaluations with evidence. However, the evaluations may not be as thoughtful as those of exemplary readers. The student may challenge the text by disagreeing with or questioning the author.

SCORE 6   EXEMPLARY READING PERFORMANCE

The student displays a perceptive and insightful understanding of the whole text and an awareness of how the parts work together to create the whole. Responses exhibit higher-order processing. The student may use text difficulties (e.g., ambiguities, contradictions) as a springboard to deeper meaning.

The student displays exceptional reflective thinking about the text, expresses significant insight regarding the text as a whole (e.g., theme, point of view), generalizes beyond the text, demonstrates emotional and/or intellectual engagement with the text, and generally searches for a deeper understanding of the text.

The student displays persuasive associations between the text and other texts, other media, and/or personal experience, and supports those associations with strong and compelling evidence. The student uses personal knowledge to interpret the text and arrives at new or clarified understandings of human nature.

The student displays sensitivity to linguistic, cultural, and psychological features of the text; makes thoughtful judgments about the literary quality of the text; and supports those judgments with evidence from the text and/or personal experience. Responses show evidence that the student has engaged in reflective reading (e.g., by agreeing or disagreeing with the author and/or raising questions).

SCORING THE WRITING SECTION

The **Writing** section of the integrated performance assessment is linked to the **Reading section** in one of two ways. Most of the writing assessments are linked to the topic or theme of the reading selection. In these assessments, students may use the reading selection as a springboard for writing a piece based on prior knowledge and experience. Other writing assessments require the student to write an interpretation or evaluation of the reading selection itself. In these assessments, the writing task is more closely tied to the reading selection.

Two holistic judgments are made in scoring the student's writing—one for Rhetorical Effectiveness and one for Conventions. Each dimension is scored on a 6-point scale. Rhetorical Effectiveness assesses the student's ability to communicate using the particular features of the writing form being assessed. Conventions assesses the student's proficiency in using correct grammar, punctuation, capitalization, and spelling.

SCORING RUBRICS FOR WRITING

Rubrics are provided to guide the scoring of a student's writing. The rubrics for Rhetorical Effectiveness are specifically linked to the particular writing form that is being assessed (e.g., report of information, autobiographical incident) and will therefore vary from assessment to assessment. The rubric for Conventions remains the same for all assessments. Rubrics for scoring Rhetorical Effectiveness and Conventions can be found in the **Appendix.** Model papers are also provided in the **Appendix** to illustrate various levels of performance in both Rhetorical Effectiveness and Conventions.

In scoring a student's writing, the teacher should ask two questions. *How well did the student communicate?* and *How well did the student use the conventions of written language?* To answer the first question, the rubric for Rhetorical Effectiveness should be used. To answer the second question, the rubric for Conventions should be used. These should be independent judgments. That is, features such as misspellings and grammatical errors, which fall under the rubric of Conventions, should not influence the score given in Rhetorical Effectiveness. Likewise, features such as development and support should not influence the score given in Conventions.

CUSTOMIZING THE SCORING SYSTEM

The scoring system used for the integrated performance assessments is designed to be compatible with many state assessment programs. Therefore, a 6-point scale was selected and is used consistently across all three areas that are scored—Reading, Rhetorical Effectiveness, and Conventions.

Some teachers, however, may desire a simpler scoring method that doesn't require making subtle distinctions between score points. For those teachers, a 3-point scale might be more appropriate. It is relatively easy to make the transition from the 6-point scale provided with the integrated performance assessments to a 3-point scale for classroom use. The following graphic illustrates the relationship between the two scales.

6-POINT SCALE					
Minimal Achievement	Limited Achievement	Some Achievement	Adequate Achievement	Commendable Achievement	Exceptional Achievement
1	2	3	4	5	6

3-POINT SCALE		
Limited Achievement	Adequate Achievement	Excellent Achievement
1	2	3

In using the 3-point scale, the teacher classifies the student's performance as "limited," "adequate," or "excellent." Papers that would be 1's and 2's on the 6-point scale become 1's; papers that would be 3's and 4's become 2's; and papers that would be 5's and 6's become 3's.

INTERPRETING AND SHARING
PERFORMANCE ASSESSMENT RESULTS

The integrated performance assessments can provide valuable insights into students' language arts abilities by revealing how all students performed on a common task. However, it is important that performance on the assessments be interpreted in light of other reading, writing, speaking, and listening samples that have been collected. It is the range of language arts activities that students engage in that will provide the most valid understanding of their abilities and the most useful information for planning instruction.

Three sources of information that are helpful in planning instruction can be derived from the integrated performance assessments:

- the students' final products (i.e., the cumulative reading responses and the final draft in writing)
- the students' marginal notes in reading, prewriting notes, and preliminary drafts
- observations recorded while students were working on the assessments

Scoring a student's final reading responses and final draft in writing represents a type of "product evaluation." On the other hand, reviewing margin notes, prewriting notes, preliminary drafts, and observational checklists is a type of "process evaluation." When these two approaches to assessment are combined, a more thorough and comprehensive understanding of student performance is possible.

SHARING RESULTS WITH STUDENTS

If the integrated performance assessments are presented as "informal activities" rather than tests, students will gain instructional benefit from them. Listed below are some suggestions for sharing results with students.

1. Discuss the rubrics with students. Distribute copies of the rubrics for **Reading, Rhetorical Effectiveness,** and **Conventions.** Explain how the rubric is used. Show students the standards used to judge responses. You may even want to score some anonymous papers as a group, or have students score each other's papers and discuss the criteria as they apply to those papers.

2. Make photocopies of the rubrics and use them as individual score reports. As you score each student's paper, circle your rating on the rubric, make marginal comments, and circle or highlight the parts of the rubric that apply to the student's response. Discuss the reports in conferences with students, pointing out their strengths as well as areas where they could still improve.

3. After students have completed an integrated performance assessment, share the model papers with them. Show the model papers without scores. Ask students what they like and don't like about the papers.

SHARING RESULTS WITH PARENTS

Results of the integrated performance assessments may also be shared with parents. Parents will appreciate seeing what their children can do on performance-based reading and writing tasks. Listed below are some suggestions for parent-teacher conferences.

1. Show parents the integrated performance assessment so they understand the task that their student was asked to perform.

2. Show parents the child's responses, and discuss the strengths and weaknesses of

the responses. Explain the scoring rubric and how the responses were evaluated.

3. Show parents the model papers to illustrate the range in student performance that is possible on this performance task. Compare their child's paper with the model papers to help put their student's paper in perspective.

4. Explain what kinds of activities they can do at home to foster greater interest in reading and writing.

USING RESULTS TO ASSIGN GRADES

Even though instructional practices are changing and new forms of assessment are emerging, most teachers are still faced with the task of giving grades. Although many teachers would prefer not to give grades, school districts and parents often insist on numerical or letter grades. The challenge is to find thoughtful ways of matching new instructional practices and assessments with more traditional requirements.

No single test, whether it is a standardized achievement test, a performance assessment, or an open-ended test, can fully measure a student's reading and writing ability. For this reason, it is important to use multiple measures of assessment.

Integrated performance assessment offers a unique approach to assessing reading and writing, but like any other form of assessment, the process has limitations. For example, a student's reading ability is assessed here by evaluating what that student writes. However, some students may perform differently if asked to answer multiple-choice questions or to discuss a literature selection. Furthermore, the writing that students do on the integrated performance assessments is somewhat constrained by the topic and writing prompt. Some students might perform differently on self-selected topics.

Therefore, it is important for the scores obtained on integrated performance assessments not to be used as the sole determiner of a report card grade or semester grade.

Optimally, the integrated performance assessments could represent one of several factors used to determine a student's grade. Those assessments could be combined with the results of selection tests, daily work samples, class participation, self-reflections, and various writing samples collected in a portfolio. However, if the responses to the integrated performance assessments do contribute to the grade awarded for a grading period, the following table is illustrative of how holistic scores can be converted into numerical or letter grades. The ranges in the table could be adjusted depending on local needs.

Holistic Score	Letter Grade	Numerical Grade
6	A	96 – 100
5	A	90 – 95
4	B	80 – 89
3	C	70 – 79
2	D	60 – 69
1	F	59 and below

APPENDIX

ABBREVIATED RUBRIC FOR SCORING READING

SCORE ❶ Minimal Reading Performance

The student
- displays minimal understanding and/or serious misunderstanding of the text
- exhibits no reflective thinking about the text and focuses on parts of the text rather than the whole
- makes no meaningful associations between the text and personal experience
- shows no ability to make meaningful, critical judgments about the text or sensitivity to aesthetic features

SCORE ❷ Limited Reading Performance

The student
- displays limited or superficial understanding of the text
- exhibits little, if any, reflective thinking about the text and simplistic expressions of major understandings (e.g., theme, point of view)
- has difficulty making meaningful associations between the text and personal experience
- shows limited ability to critically evaluate the text and little, if any, sensitivity to aesthetic features

SCORE ❸ Literal Reading Performance

The student
- displays a plausible but simplistic, literal understanding of the text
- exhibits little reflective thinking about the text and predictable expressions of major themes
- makes superficial associations between the text and personal experience that lack depth of understanding and support
- shows limited or superficial evaluative judgments of the text and limited aesthetic appreciation

SCORE ❹ Thoughtful Reading Performance

The student
- displays a thoughtful understanding of the whole text
- exhibits some reflective thinking about the text and attempts to express a personal interpretation that goes beyond the literal understanding
- makes routine and predictable associations between the text and personal experience
- shows some ability to critically evaluate the text and/or displays aesthetic appreciation

SCORE ❺ Discerning Reading Performance

The student
- displays a thoughtful and perceptive understanding of the whole text
- exhibits considerable reflective thinking about the text but lacks the deeper interpretations exhibited by superior readers
- makes thoughtful associations between the text and personal experience
- makes critical judgments of the text and shows sensitivity to linguistic, cultural, and psychological features of the text

SCORE ❻ Exemplary Reading Performance

The student
- displays perceptive and insightful understanding of the whole text
- exhibits exceptional reflective thinking about the text
- makes persuasive associations between the text and personal experience that are supported with strong and compelling evidence
- makes thoughtful judgments about the literary quality of the text that are supported with evidence from the text and/or personal experience

ASSESSMENT • 1

SCORING RUBRIC FOR RHETORICAL EFFECTIVENESS IN OBSERVATIONAL ESSAY

SCORE ❶ Minimal Evidence of Achievement

In this response emphasis is on the observer, rather than on the subject or subjects being observed. The writer does not provide a context for the observation. Little or no information about the subject is presented, or the information is unclear. The writer does not convey the meaning or importance of the observation to the reader.

SCORE ❷ Limited Evidence of Achievement

The writer may provide minimal context for the observation, but tends to emphasize the observer rather than the subject being observed. Multiple subjects may be introduced. Information about the subject is superficial and general. There is no evidence of why the observation is meaningful or significant.

SCORE ❸ Some Evidence of Achievement

The writer provides some context for the observation but may allow the context to dominate the subject. Information about the subject tends to be general rather than specific. The point of view may shift or change throughout the paper. The writer does not address the meaning or importance of the subject and shows little awareness of the reader.

SCORE ❹ Adequate Achievement

The writer clearly identifies the subject and provides a context for the observation. Enough detailed information about the subject is provided to enable the reader to grasp the essence of the experience. The writer may attempt to convey the significance of the experience, but does not fully succeed. The point of view may unintentionally shift throughout the paper.

SCORE ❺ Commendable Achievement

The writer places the subject in a specific physical context that serves to ground the reader. The relationship between the writer (observer) and the subject is well established. Sufficient detailed information about the subject is provided to enable the reader to re-create and appreciate the observation. A consistent point of view is maintained.

SCORE ❻ Exceptional Achievement

The writer clearly identifies or defines the subject and places it in a specific physical or psychological context. The relationship between the writer and the subject is clearly established. The writer assumes an authoritative stance and conveys a sense of discovery about the experience. The point of view may shift deliberately to show different perspectives. The writer enables the reader to see the scene clearly and to understand the importance of the experience to the writer.

ASSESSMENT • 2

SCORING RUBRIC FOR RHETORICAL EFFECTIVENESS IN PERSUASIVE ESSAY

SCORE **1** Minimal Evidence of Achievement

The writer may not state the issue to be addressed or orient the reader to the issue. No position is stated and support is missing. The response is characterized by confusion or uncertainty about the issue or task.

SCORE **2** Limited Evidence of Achievement

The writer may only mention the issue without orienting readers. If a position is taken on the issue, it is not clear and may be changed or abandoned as the response is developed. Support is illogical, irrelevant, vague, or superficial. Repetitions and digressions may disrupt the flow of the response.

SCORE **3** Some Evidence of Achievement

The writer may offer a brief explanation of the issue to help orient the reader. A stand is taken but it may lack consistency. The writer offers support but fails to elaborate and link the support to form a central thesis. Counterarguments may not be acknowledged. The arguments the writer presents are not very convincing.

SCORE **4** Adequate Achievement

The writer states the issue but may not orient the reader. A clear stance or position is taken, but it may lack authority and conviction. Supporting evidence is presented but it may not be as thoughtful, extensive, or convincing as that found in papers receiving higher scores. Overall, the response may lack unity and a central theme.

SCORE **5** Commendable Achievement

The writer orients the reader by setting the issue in a meaningful context. A firm and clear position is taken and maintained thoughout the response. Support is thoughtful and elaborated. Counterarguments are acknowledged but may not be effectively refuted. The overall tone is reasonable, appropriate, and convincing.

SCORE **6** Exceptional Achievement

The writer orients the reader by clearly defining and framing the issue. A firm, authoritative stand is taken and maintained. In offering support, the writer may use a variety of strategies to build a unified, central thesis that represents perceptive thinking about the issue. Counterarguments are acknowledged and effectively refuted. Overall, the response is convincing and engaging.

ASSESSMENT • 3

SCORING RUBRIC FOR RHETORICAL EFFECTIVENESS IN INTERPRETIVE ESSAY

SCORE **1** **Minimal Evidence of Achievement**

The writer only briefly describes the subject and may fail to place the subject in context. No interpretation is made. Rather, the writer may merely summarize or retell the selection at a literal level. The response is missing supportive evidence, and the writer may display a lack of understanding either of the passage or the interpretive task.

SCORE **2** **Limited Evidence of Achievement**

The writer may simply identify the subject and/or offer a brief introduction. If interpretive claims are made they tend to be obvious, broad, and general. There may be some evidence of understanding beyond the literal level, but the response lacks thoughtful interpretation and supporting evidence. The writer has difficulty making interpretive claims.

SCORE **3** **Some Evidence of Achievement**

The writer may offer a brief introduction that contextualizes the subject. Interpretive claims are obvious. An attempt is made to offer supporting evidence, but the writer may resort to summarizing the passage or may not adequately develop the evidence presented. The response may show some interpretation, but the writer lacks control and is unaware of the reader's needs.

SCORE **4** **Adequate Achievement**

The writer introduces the subject and orients the reader to the interpretation. At least one interpretive claim is made but it may be predictable and lack insight. Alternatively, several claims are made but they are not related or linked in a meaningful way. Relevant evidence is provided to support the interpretation, but the evidence tends to be general, lacking in specific, detailed support.

SCORE **5** **Commendable Achievement**

The writer introduces the subject, provides context, and explicitly forecasts the claim(s) that will be made. The interpretation is clear and insightful. The writer presents substantial evidence that is relevant, detailed, and convincing. The writer displays authority and control.

SCORE **6** **Exceptional Achievement**

The writer introduces the subject and provides the reader with a context in which to follow the interpretation. Interpretive claims are thoughtful and perceptive and go beyond the predictable. The interpretation is skillfully supported with various types of evidence. The response is fully developed and complete. The writer displays authority and a commitment to convince readers of the interpretation.

ASSESSMENT • 4

SCORING RUBRIC FOR RHETORICAL EFFECTIVENESS IN EVALUATION

SCORE ① Minimal Evidence of Achievement

The writer only briefly describes the subject and may fail to contextualize it for the reader. A judgment may be stated but supporting evidence is extremely brief and superficial, and is usually based on personal opinion. The writer displays no conviction or personal involvement with the subject.

SCORE ② Limited Evidence of Achievement

The writer states a judgment but may fail to provide meaningful reasons for supporting the judgment, or else provides a list of undeveloped, sometimes irrelevant, reasons. The writer may focus more on describing and summarizing the subject. Little conviction or personal involvement is evident.

SCORE ③ Some Evidence of Achievement

The writer states a judgment and gives one or more reasons in support of the judgment. However, the reasons may be listed only and not fully developed. The reasons tend to be predictable and reveal little insight. The writer may show some personal involvement with the subject, but the involvement is not convincing.

SCORE ④ Adequate Achievement

The writer introduces the subject before stating a clear judgment. The judgment is supported by meaningful reasons, some of which are moderately developed. The response is likely to lack balance; the writer may spend too much time describing the subject at the expense of supporting the judgment. Reasons are logical but lack the freshness and perception seen in higher achievement levels.

SCORE ⑤ Commendable Achievement

The writer identifies the subject and provides a firm judgment. The judgment is supported by meaningful reasons that are well developed. The response presents a unified, convincing argument. The writer exhibits confidence and authority but may lack the originality and perception found in higher achievement levels.

SCORE ⑥ Exceptional Achievement

The writer names or identifies the subject and then establishes a firm, clear judgment about it. The judgment is often expressed in a fresh, original way. One or more reasons are offered in support of the judgment, and some of the reasons are supported with examples or evidence. Support is insightful and perceptive. The writer displays a clear sense of conviction and personal involvement. Overall, the response exhibits a sense of direction, purpose, movement, and closure.

GENERAL SCORING RUBRIC FOR CONVENTIONS
USED WITH ALL ASSESSMENT FORMS

SCORE 1 MINIMAL EVIDENCE OF ACHIEVEMENT

The response demonstrates great difficulty in applying the conventions of language. The writer seems unaware of acceptable standards in mechanics, usage, or spelling. Frequent and serious errors may make the response incoherent or incomprehensible.

SCORE 2 LIMITED EVIDENCE OF ACHIEVEMENT

The response displays very limited ability to use the conventions of language. Errors in mechanics, usage, or spelling are frequent and serious. Many of the errors make the response difficult to read and interpret.

SCORE 3 SOME EVIDENCE OF ACHIEVEMENT

The response demonstrates marginally successful use of the conventions of language. Patterns of errors in mechanics, usage, or spelling are likely to be evident. Several errors may be serious and disrupt the meaning of the response.

SCORE 4 ADEQUATE ACHIEVEMENT

The response displays reasonable use of the conventions of language, but contains some errors in mechanics, usage, or spelling. Most of the errors are minor, but a few may be serious. The mistakes generally do not interfere with communication.

SCORE 5 COMMENDABLE ACHIEVEMENT

The response demonstrates successful use of the conventions of language, but may contain a few errors in mechanics, usage, or spelling. If present, the errors are relatively minor and do not interfere with communication.

SCORE 6 EXCEPTIONAL ACHIEVEMENT

The response displays exceptional command of the conventions of language and is likely to be error-free. Errors in mechanics, usage, and spelling are extremely rare and do not interfere with communication.

COPYING MASTERS OF STUDENT ASSESSMENT FORMS

ASSESSMENT • 1

LEVEL F

NAME _____

CLASS _____

DATE _____

INTEGRATED
PERFORMANCE ASSESSMENT
STUDENT FORMS

ASSESSMENT • 1

READING SECTION

➤ Directions:

Today you will read a poem. Then you will write about what you have read. You should write down your thoughts, questions, and opinions as you read. Your notes will help you when you write about the poem. When you finish reading, answer all of the questions about the poem until you come to the word STOP.

Getting Ready to Read

The following poem was written in 1678 by the Puritan poet Anne Bradstreet. One of the early Massachusetts Bay colonists, Bradstreet produced the first book of poems written in English in the Americas. Bradstreet's poems were published in London by her brother-in-law, apparently without her knowledge or consent. The poem you are about to read was probably written when she was revising her book for a second printing.

Time to Read

The Author to Her Book
by
Anne Bradstreet

My thoughts about what I am reading

Thou ill-formed offspring of my feeble brain,
Who after birth didst by my side remain,
Till snatched from thence by friends, less wise than true,
Who thee abroad, exposed to public view,
Made thee in rags, halting to th' press to trudge,
Where errors were not lessened (all may judge).
At thy return my blushing was not small,
My rambling brat (in print) should mother call,
I cast thee by as one unfit for light,
Thy visage was so irksome in my sight;
Yet being mine own, at length affection would
Thy blemishes amend, if so I could:
I washed thy face, but more defects I saw,
And rubbing off a spot still made a flaw.
I stretched thy joints to make thee even feet,[1]
Yet still thou run'st more hobbling than is meet;[2]
In better dress to trim thee was my mind,
But nought save homespun cloth i' th' house I find.

---

1. **even feet:** metrical feet; to even out the pattern of stressed and unstressed syllables in the poem.
2. **meet:** appropriate or pleasing.

GO ON

In this array 'mongst vulgars[3] may'st thou roam.
In critic's hands beware thou dost not come,
And take thy way where yet thou art not known
If for thy father asked, say thou hadst none;
And for thy mother, she alas is poor,
Which caused her thus to send thee out of door.

My thoughts about
what I am reading

3. **vulgars:** common people.

Responding to the Selection

Now that you have read the poem, respond to the following items as completely as possible.

1. Take a few minutes to write down your first response to the poem.

_____

_____

_____

_____

_____

_____

_____

_____

_____

_____

_____

_____

_____

_____

_____

_____

_____

_____

_____

_____

_____

_____

_____

_____

| GO ON |

2. In the box below, draw a picture of some of the images Bradstreet's poem brings to your mind.

On the lines below, explain the drawing or drawings you put in the box.

_____

_____

_____

_____

_____

_____

_____

_____

_____

_____

GO ON

3. Bradstreet uses an extended *analogy* to express her feelings about her book. An analogy compares two basically different things to show their similarities. In this poem, Bradstreet compares her book to a child. What does this analogy make you think about Bradstreet's attitude toward her book?

_____

_____

_____

_____

_____

_____

_____

_____

_____

_____

_____

_____

_____

_____

_____

_____

_____

_____

_____

_____

GO ON

4. Think of another work (a song, story or novel, movie, TV show, or painting) that also deals with the theme of creativity. Describe the work and then tell how it is similar to or different from Bradstreet's poem.

_____

_____

_____

_____

_____

_____

_____

_____

_____

5. Use this space to write down any additional thoughts you have about the poem. Tell anything else about your understanding of the poem and what it means to you.

_____

_____

_____

_____

_____

_____

_____

_____

_____

_____

_____

> **STOP!**
> **DO NOT CONTINUE UNTIL INSTRUCTED**
> **This is the end of the Reading Section**

ASSESSMENT • 1

WRITING SECTION

Getting Ready to Write

You are going to write an observational essay for your local newspaper about someone you think is creative. This should be a real person you have observed making or doing something creative.

Think of a creative person you could write about. Who is that person? What does that person look like and how does he or she behave? What makes that person creative? What special qualities does that person possess? Use the chart below to list some of your ideas before you begin writing.

Person I could write about:
Description of that person:
Creative characteristics of that person:
Special qualities of that person:

GO ON

Sharing Your Plans With Others (Optional)

Before you begin writing, share your writing plans with some of your classmates. Using your notes, tell them about the person you plan to write about. Ask your classmates questions like the following:

- Have I selected an interesting person to write about?
- Have I considered multiple ways of describing that person (for example, physical characteristics, social characteristics)?
- Have I included good examples that show that this person is creative?

Jot down reactions from your classmates in the space below.

_____

_____

_____

_____

_____

_____

_____

_____

_____

_____

_____

_____

_____

_____

_____

You should also be prepared to give comments and suggestions about your classmates' writing plans. Try to give them honest and specific suggestions. Tell them about things they may want to delete or add. Suggest ways they can organize their ideas.

GO ON

Thinking About Reactions

Spend a few minutes thinking about the comments and suggestions your classmates gave you. Review the notes you took when you met with them. Are there any changes you should make, based on their comments? Use the space below to write down any important ideas you received from your classmates or to revise your original writing plans.

_____

_____

_____

_____

_____

_____

_____

_____

_____

_____

_____

_____

_____

_____

_____

_____

_____

_____

GO ON

Time to Write

You have a summer job working as an intern reporter at your local newspaper. Your editor has asked you to write an article about someone in your community who does something creative. You are free to write about anyone you choose. Your editor has told you that she wants an eyewitness account of what the person looks like while he or she is making or doing something creative. Be sure to use physically descriptive words and analogies to give your readers a good sense of what the person does and where she or he does it. Think of yourself as a camera, using words to take a picture.

_____

_____

_____

_____

_____

_____

_____

_____

_____

_____

_____

_____

_____

_____

_____

_____

_____

_____

_____

_____

_____

_____

NAME_____ CLASS _____ DATE _____

_____

_____

_____

_____

_____

_____

_____

_____

_____

_____

_____

_____

_____

_____

_____

_____

_____

_____

_____

_____

_____

_____

_____

ASSESSMENT • 2

LEVEL F

NAME _____

CLASS _____

DATE _____

INTEGRATED
PERFORMANCE ASSESSMENT
STUDENT FORMS

ASSESSMENT • 2

READING SECTION

► Directions:

Today you will read a short story. Then you will write about what you have read. You should write down your thoughts, questions, and opinions as you read. Your notes will help you when you write about the story. When you finish reading, answer all of the questions about the story until you come to the word STOP.

Getting Ready to Read

The word *masque* in the title of this story refers to a masked ball. It also refers to a mask that disguises the face. To understand what is happening in this story on a literal level, think about the Black Death, or bubonic plague, which was an epidemic that killed seventy-five percent of the population of Europe during the fourteenth century.

Time to Read

The Masque of the Red Death
by
Edgar Allan Poe

> My thoughts about
> what I am reading

The "Red Death" had long devastated the country. No pestilence had ever been so fatal, or so hideous. Blood was its Avatar[1] and its seal—the redness and the horror of blood. There were sharp pains, and sudden dizziness, and then profuse bleeding at the pores, with dissolution. The scarlet stains upon the body and especially upon the face of the victim, were the pest ban which shut him out from the aid and from the sympathy of his fellow men. And the whole seizure, progress, and termination of the disease, were the incidents of half an hour.

But the Prince Prospero was happy and dauntless and sagacious. When his dominions were half depopulated, he summoned to his presence a thousand hale and lighthearted friends from among the knights and dames of his court, and with these retired to the deep seclusion of one of his castellated[2] abbeys. This was an extensive and magnificent structure, the creation of the prince's own eccentric yet august taste. A strong and lofty wall girdled it in. This wall had gates of iron. The courtiers, having entered, brought furnaces and massy[3] hammers and welded the bolts. They resolved to leave means neither of ingress or egress to the sudden impulses of despair or of frenzy from within. The abbey was amply provisioned. With such precautions the

---

1. **Avatar** (av'ə·tär'): a sign of an invisible force; an embodiment or manifestation.
2. **castellated** (kas'tə·lā'tid): having towers like that of a castle.
3. **massy:** here, massive.

GO ON

courtiers might bid defiance to contagion. The external world could take care of itself. In the meantime it was folly to grieve, or to think. The prince had provided all the appliances of pleasure. There were buffoons, there were improvisatori,[4] there were ballet dancers, there were musicians, there was Beauty, there was wine. All these and security were within. Without was the "Red Death."

It was toward the close of the fifth or sixth month of his seclusion, and while the pestilence raged most furiously abroad, that the Prince Prospero entertained his thousand friends at a masked ball of the most unusual magnificence.

It was a voluptuous scene, that masquerade. But first let me tell of the rooms in which it was held. There were seven—an imperial suite. In many palaces, however, such suites form a long and straight vista, while the folding doors slide back nearly to the walls on either hand, so that the view of the whole extent is scarcely impeded. Here the case was very different; as might have been expected from the duke's love of the *bizarre*. The apartments were so irregularly disposed that the vision embraced but little more than one at a time. There was a sharp turn at every twenty or thirty yards, and at each turn a novel effect. To the right and left, in the middle of each wall, a tall and narrow Gothic window looked out upon a closed corridor which pursued the windings of the suite. These windows were of stained glass whose color varied in accordance with the prevailing hue of the decorations of the chamber into which it opened. That at the eastern extremity was hung, for example, in blue—and vividly blue were its windows. The second chamber was purple in its ornaments and tapestries, and here the panes were purple. The third was green throughout, and so were the casements. The fourth was furnished and lighted with orange—the fifth with white—the sixth with violet. The seventh apartment was closely shrouded in black velvet tapestries that hung all over the ceiling and down the walls, falling in heavy folds upon a carpet of the same material and hue. But in this chamber only, the color of the windows failed to correspond with the decorations. The panes here were scarlet—a deep blood color. Now in no one of the seven apartments was there any lamp or candelabrum, amid the profusion of golden ornaments that lay scattered to and fro or depended from the roof. There was no light of any kind emanating from lamp or candle within the suite of chambers. But in the corridors that followed the suite, there stood, opposite to each window, a heavy tripod, bearing a brazier of fire that projected its rays through the tinted glass and so glaringly illumined the room. And thus were produced a multitude of gaudy and fantastic appearances. But in the western or black chamber the effect of the firelight

> My thoughts about what I am reading

---

4. **improvisatori** (im·präv'ə·zə·tōr'ē): performers who improvise scenes at the suggestions of onlookers.

GO ON

that streamed upon the dark hangings through the blood-tinted panes was ghastly in the extreme, and produced so wild a look upon the countenances of those who entered, that there were few of the company bold enough to set foot within its precincts at all.

It was in this apartment, also, that there stood against the western wall, a gigantic clock of ebony. Its pendulum swung to and fro with a dull, heavy, monotonous clang; and when the minute hand made the circuit of the face, and the hour was to be stricken, there came from the brazen lungs of the clock a sound which was clear and loud and deep and exceedingly musical, but of so peculiar a note and emphasis that, at each lapse of an hour, the musicians of the orchestra were constrained to pause, momentarily, in their performance, to hearken to the sound; and thus the waltzers perforce ceased their evolutions; and there was a brief disconcert of the whole gay company; and, while the chimes of the clock yet rang, it was observed that the giddiest grew pale, and the more aged and sedate passed their hands over their brows as if in confused reverie or meditation. But when the echoes had fully ceased, a light laughter at once pervaded the assembly; the musicians looked at each other and smiled as if at their own nervousness and folly, and made whispering vows, each to the other, that the next chiming of the clock should produce in them no similar emotion; and then, after the lapse of sixty minutes (which embrace three thousand and six hundred seconds of the Time that flies), there came yet another chiming of the clock, and then were the same disconcert and tremulousness and meditation as before.

But, in spite of these things, it was a gay and magnificent revel. The tastes of the duke were peculiar. He had a fine eye for colors and effects. He disregarded the *decora*[5] of mere fashion. His plans were bold and fiery, and his conceptions glowed with barbaric luster. There are some who would have thought him mad. His followers felt that he was not. It was necessary to hear and see and touch him to be *sure* that he was not.

He had directed, in great part, the moveable embellishments of the seven chambers, upon occasion of this great *fête;* and it was his own guiding taste which had given character to the masqueraders. Be sure they were grotesque. There were much glare and glitter and piquancy and phantasm—much of what has been since seen in *Hernani.*[6] There were arabesque figures with unsuited limbs and appointments. There were delirious fancies such as the madman fashions. There was much of the beautiful, much of the wanton, much of the *bizarre,* something of the terrible, and not a

> My thoughts about what I am reading

---

5. *decora* (dā·kôr′ä): Latin for "dictates"; here, proper good taste.
6. *Hernani* (er·nä′nē): a romantic stage tragedy by the French writer Victor Hugo (1802–1885), first presented in 1830.

GO ON

little of that which might have excited disgust. To and fro in the seven chambers there stalked, in fact, a multitude of dreams. And these—the dreams—writhed in and about, taking hue from the rooms, and causing the wild music of the orchestra to seem as the echo of their steps. And, anon, there strikes the ebony clock which stands in the hall of the velvet. And then, for a moment, all is still, and all is silent save the voice of the clock. The dreams are stiff-frozen as they stand. But the echoes of the chime die away—they have endured but an instant—and a light, half-subdued laughter floats after them as they depart. And now again the music swells, and the dreams live, and writhe to and fro more merrily than ever, taking hue from the many-tinted windows through which stream the rays from the tripods. But to the chamber which lies most westwardly of the seven, there are now none of the maskers who venture; for the night is waning away; and there flows a ruddier light through the blood-colored panes; and the blackness of the sable drapery appalls; and to him whose foot falls upon the sable carpet, there comes from the near clock of ebony a muffled peal more solemnly emphatic than any which reaches *their* ears who indulge in the more remote gaieties of the other apartments.

But these other apartments were densely crowded, and in them beat feverishly the heart of life. And the revel went whirlingly on, until at length there commenced the sounding of midnight upon the clock. And then the music ceased, as I have told; and the evolutions of the waltzers were quieted; and there was an uneasy cessation of all things as before. But now there were twelve strokes to be sounded by the bell of the clock; and thus it happened, perhaps, that more of thought crept, with more of time, into the meditations of the thoughtful among those who reveled. And thus, too, it happened, perhaps, that before the last echoes of the last chime had utterly sunk into silence, there were many individuals in the crowd who had found leisure to become aware of the presence of a masked figure which had arrested the attention of no single individual before. And the rumor of this new presence having spread itself whisperingly around, there arose at length from the whole company a buzz, or murmur, expressive of disapprobation and surprise—then, finally, of terror, of horror, and of disgust.

In an assembly of phantasms such as I have painted, it may well be supposed that no ordinary appearance could have excited such sensation. In truth the masquerade license of the night was nearly unlimited; but, the figure in question

My thoughts about what I am reading

GO ON

My thoughts about
what I am reading

had out-Heroded Herod,[7] and gone beyond the bounds of even the prince's indefinite decorum. There are chords in the hearts of the most reckless which cannot be touched without emotion. Even with the utterly lost, to whom life and death are equally jests, there are matters of which no jest can be made. The whole company, indeed, seemed now deeply to feel that in the costume and bearing of the stranger neither wit nor propriety existed. The figure was tall and gaunt, and shrouded from head to foot in the habiliments of the grave. The mask which concealed the visage was made so nearly to resemble the countenance of a stiffened corpse that the closest scrutiny must have had difficulty in detecting the cheat. And yet all this might have been endured, if not approved, by the mad revelers around. But the mummer[8] had gone so far as to assume the type of the Red Death. His vesture was dabbled in *blood*—and his broad brow, with all the features of the face, was besprinkled with the scarlet horror.

When the eyes of Prince Prospero fell upon this spectral image (which with a slow and solemn movement, as if more fully to sustain its *rôle*, stalked to and fro among the waltzers) he was seen to be convulsed, in the first moment with a strong shudder either of terror or distaste; but, in the next, his brow reddened with rage.

"Who dares?" he demanded hoarsely of the courtiers who stood near him—"who dares insult us with this blasphemous mockery? Seize him and unmask him—that we may know whom we have to hang at sunrise, from the battlements!"

It was in the eastern or blue chamber in which stood the Prince Prospero as he uttered these words. They rang throughout the seven rooms loudly and clearly—for the prince was a bold and robust man, and the music had become hushed at the waving of his hand.

It was in the blue room where stood the prince, with a group of pale courtiers by his side. At first, as he spoke, there was a slight rushing movement of this group in the direction of the intruder, who at the moment was also near at hand, and now, with deliberate and stately step, made closer approach to the speaker. But from a certain nameless awe with which the mad assumptions of the mummer had inspired the whole party, there were found none who put forth hand to seize him; so that, unimpeded, he passed within a yard of the prince's person; and, while the vast

---

7. **out-Heroded Herod:** had acted in extreme, perhaps crazed fashion. The Biblical king Herod sought to destroy the infant Jesus by ordering the slaughter of all children in Judea. He was depicted in later times as a raging, sometimes demented figure. Shakespeare uses the phrase in *Hamlet* (III, 2) for overacting.
8. **mummer:** masked person.

GO ON

assembly, as if with one impulse, shrank from the centers of the rooms to the walls, he made his way uninterruptedly, but with the same solemn and measured step which had distinguished him from the first, through the blue chamber to the purple—through the purple to the green—through the green to the orange—through this again to the white— and even thence to the violet, ere a decided movement had been made to arrest him. It was then, however, that the Prince Prospero, maddening with rage and the shame of his own momentary cowardice, rushed hurriedly through the six chambers, while none followed him on account of a deadly terror that had seized upon all. He bore aloft a drawn dagger, and had approached, in rapid impetuosity, to within three or four feet of the retreating figure, when the latter, having attained the extremity of the velvet apartment, turned suddenly and confronted his pursuer. There was a sharp cry—and the dagger dropped gleaming upon the sable carpet, upon which, instantly afterward, fell prostrate in death the Prince Prospero. Then, summoning the wild courage of despair, a throng of the revelers at once threw themselves into the black apartment, and seizing the mummer, whose tall figure stood erect and motionless within the shadow of the ebony clock, gasped in unutterable horror at finding the grave-cerements[9] and corpselike mask which they handled with so violent a rudeness, untenanted by any tangible form.

And now was acknowledged the presence of the Red Death. He had come like a thief in the night.[10] And one by one dropped the revelers in the blood-bedewed halls of their revel, and died each in the despairing posture of his fall. And the life of the ebony clock went out with that of the last of the gay. And the flames of the tripods expired. And Darkness and Decay and the Red Death held illimitable dominion over all.

My thoughts about what I am reading

---

9. **grave-cerements:** shrouds or clothes used in covering a corpse.
10. **a thief in the night:** A Biblical reference to I Thessalonians 5:2–3, signi-
   fying swift and unexpected death: "For yourselves know perfectly that
   the day of the Lord so cometh as a thief in the night.
   "For when they shall say, Peace and safety; the sudden destruction
   cometh upon them, as travail upon a woman with child; and they shall
   not escape."

GO ON

Responding to the Selection

Now that you have read the story, respond to the following items as completely as possible.

1. Take a few minutes to write down your first response to the story.

_____

_____

_____

_____

_____

_____

_____

_____

2. If Prince Prospero were to tell you about his philosophy of life, what do you think he would say? What makes you think so?

_____

_____

_____

_____

_____

_____

_____

_____

_____

_____

| GO ON |

3. Read the following passage from the story and then write your opinions of the attitudes expressed in it.

> The courtiers, having entered, brought furnaces and massy hammers and welded the bolts. They resolved to leave means neither of ingress or egress to the sudden impulses of despair or of frenzy from within. The abbey was amply provisioned. With such precautions the courtiers might bid defiance to contagion. The external world could take care of itself. In the meantime it was folly to grieve, or to think.

_____

_____

_____

_____

_____

_____

_____

_____

_____

_____

_____

_____

_____

_____

_____

_____

_____

_____

_____

_____

GO ON

4. Suppose you were planning to make a movie version of "The Masque of the Red Death." Thinking about other films you have seen that have powerful opening images, write a brief description of the first image you would have appear on the screen. Why would you choose that image?

_____

_____

_____

_____

_____

_____

_____

_____

_____

_____

_____

_____

_____

_____

_____

_____

_____

_____

_____

_____

GO ON

5. Use this page to write down any additional thoughts you have about the story. Tell anything else about your understanding of the story and what it means to you.

_____

_____

_____

_____

_____

_____

_____

_____

_____

_____

_____

_____

_____

_____

_____

_____

_____

_____

_____

_____

_____

_____

_____

_____

_____

_____

STOP!
DO NOT CONTINUE UNTIL INSTRUCTED
This is the end of the Reading Section

ASSESSMENT • 2
WRITING SECTION

Getting Ready to Write

You are going to write a letter to the editor of your school newspaper about a controversial issue that affects people your age. Select an issue that is interesting and important to you. Phrase your issue as a question. (Example: "Should students be required to pass all courses in order to participate in school-sponsored extracurricular activities?")

Think of a controversial issue you could write about. What is your position on that issue? What evidence or arguments could you use to support your position? What are some counterarguments to your position? Use the chart to list some of your ideas before you begin writing.

Controversial issue I could write about:
My position on that issue:
Support for my position:
Counterarguments to my position:

GO ON

Sharing Your Plans With Others (Optional)

Before you begin writing, share your writing plans with some of your classmates. Using your notes, tell them about the controversial issue you plan to write about. Ask your classmates questions like the following:

- Have I chosen a controversial issue that is interesting and important?
- Do I have a clear position on the issue?
- Have I thought of supporting arguments for my position?
- Have I thought of likely counterarguments to my position?

Jot down reactions from your classmates in the space below.

_____

_____

_____

_____

_____

_____

_____

_____

_____

_____

_____

_____

_____

_____

_____

_____

_____

You should also be prepared to give comments and suggestions about your classmates' writing plans. Try to give them honest and specific suggestions. Tell them about things they may want to delete or add. Suggest ways they can organize their ideas.

GO ON

Thinking About Reactions

Spend a few minutes thinking about the comments and suggestions your classmates gave you. Review the notes you took when you met with them. Are there any changes you should make, based on their comments? Use the space below to write down any important ideas you received from your classmates or to revise your original writing plans.

_____

_____

_____

_____

_____

_____

_____

_____

_____

_____

_____

_____

_____

_____

_____

_____

_____

_____

_____

_____

_____

GO ON

Time to Write

You have been asked to write a letter to the editor of your school newspaper. In your letter, you will take a position on a current controversy that affects people your age, and you will try to convince your readers that your position is reasonable. Your letter should define the issue, clearly state your opinion, present likely counterarguments and refute them, and give reasonable evidence that convinces readers to support your position.

_____

_____

_____

_____

_____

_____

_____

_____

_____

_____

_____

_____

_____

_____

_____

_____

_____

_____

_____

_____

_____

_____

_____

_____

_____

_____

_____

_____

_____

_____

_____

_____

_____

_____

_____

_____

_____

_____

_____

_____

_____

_____

_____

_____

_____

_____

_____

_____

_____

_____

_____

_____

_____

_____

_____

_____

_____

_____

_____

_____

_____

_____

_____

_____

_____

_____

_____

_____

_____

_____

_____

_____

_____

_____

_____

_____

_____

_____

_____

_____

ASSESSMENT • 3

LEVEL F

NAME _____

CLASS _____

DATE _____

INTEGRATED
PERFORMANCE ASSESSMENT
STUDENT FORMS

ASSESSMENT • 3

READING SECTION

➤ Directions:

Today you will read an autobiographical essay. Then you will write about what you have read. You should write down your thoughts, questions, and opinions as you read. Your notes will help you when you write about the essay. When you finish reading, answer all of the questions about the essay until you come to the word STOP.

Getting Ready to Read

Zora Neale Hurston was born around the turn of the century and grew up in Eatonville, Florida, the first incorporated, self-governing, all–African American town in the United States. "How It Feels to Be Colored Me" will give you a glimpse of what it meant to Hurston to grow up in a town like Eatonville and to travel on from there.

Time to Read

How It Feels to Be Colored Me
by
Zora Neale Hurston

> My thoughts about what I am reading

I am colored but I offer nothing in the way of extenuating circumstances except the fact that I am the only Negro in the United States whose grandfather on the mother's side was *not* an Indian chief.

I remember the very day that I became colored. Up to my thirteenth year I lived in the little Negro town of Eatonville, Florida. It is exclusively a colored town. The only white people I knew passed through the town going to or coming from Orlando. The native whites rode dusty horses, the Northern tourists chugged down the sandy village road in automobiles. The town knew the Southerners and never stopped cane chewing[1] when they passed. But the Northerners were something else again. They were peered at cautiously from behind curtains by the timid. The more venturesome would come out on the porch to watch them go past and got just as much pleasure out of the tourists as the tourists got out of the village.

The front porch might seem a daring place for the rest of the town, but it was a gallery seat for me. My favorite place was atop the gate-post. Proscenium box for a born first-nighter. Not only did I enjoy the show, but I didn't mind the actors knowing that I liked it. I usually spoke to them in passing. I'd wave at them and when they returned my salute, I would say something like this: "Howdy-do-well-I-

---

1. **cane chewing:** chewing sugar cane.

GO ON

thank-you-where-you-goin'?" Usually automobile or the horse paused at this, and after a queer exchange of compliments, I would probably "go a piece of the way" with them, as we say in farthest Florida. If one of my family happened to come to the front in time to see me, of course negotiations would be rudely broken off. But even so, it is clear that I was the first "welcome-to-our-state" Floridian, and I hope the Miami Chamber of Commerce will please take notice.

During this period, white people differed from colored to me only in that they rode through town and never lived there. They liked to hear me "speak pieces" and sing and wanted to see me dance the parse-me-la, and gave me generously of their small silver for doing these things, which seemed strange to me for I wanted to do them so much that I needed bribing to stop. Only they didn't know it. The colored people gave no dimes. They deplored any joyful tendencies in me, but I was their Zora nevertheless. I belonged to them, to the nearby hotels, to the county— everybody's Zora.

But changes came in the family when I was thirteen, and I was sent to school in Jacksonville. I left Eatonville, the town of the oleanders, as Zora. When I disembarked from the river-boat at Jacksonville, she was no more. It seemed that I had suffered a sea change. I was not Zora of Orange County any more, I was now a little colored girl. I found it out in certain ways. In my heart as well as in the mirror, I became a fast brown—warranted not to rub nor run.

But I am not tragically colored. There is no great sorrow dammed up in my soul, nor lurking behind my eyes. I do not mind at all. I do not belong to the sobbing school of Negrohood who hold that nature somehow has given them a lowdown dirty deal and whose feelings are all hurt about it. Even in the helter-skelter skirmish that is my life, I have seen that the world is to the strong regardless of a little pigmentation more or less. No, I do not weep at the world—I am too busy sharpening my oyster knife.[2]

Someone is always at my elbow reminding me that I am the granddaughter of slaves. It fails to register depression with me. Slavery is sixty years in the past. The operation was successful and the patient is doing well, thank you. The terrible struggle[3] that made me an American out of a potential slave said "On the line!" The Reconstruction said "Get set!"; and the generation before said "Go!" I am off to a

> My thoughts about what I am reading

2. **oyster knife:** a reference to the popular expression "The world is my oyster."
3. **The terrible struggle:** i. e., the Civil War. The reconstruction was the period immediately following the war, when Northern educators traveled to the South to teach the newly freed slaves.

My thoughts about what I am reading

flying start and I must not halt in the stretch to look behind and weep. Slavery is the price I paid for civilization, and the choice was not with me. It is a bully adventure and worth all that I have paid through my ancestors for it. No one on earth ever had a greater chance for glory. The world to be won and nothing to be lost. It is thrilling to think—to know that for any act of mine, I shall get twice as much praise or twice as much blame. It is quite exciting to hold the center of the national stage, with the spectators not knowing whether to laugh or to weep.

The position of my white neighbor is much more difficult. No brown specter pulls up a chair beside me when I sit down to eat. No dark ghost thrusts its leg against mine in bed. The game of keeping what one has is never so exciting as the game of getting.

I do not always feel colored. Even now I often achieve the unconscious Zora of Eatonville before the Hegira.[4] I feel most colored when I am thrown against a sharp white background.

For instance at Barnard.[5] "Beside the waters of the Hudson" I feel my race. Among the thousand white persons, I am a dark rock surged upon, and overswept, but through it all, I remain myself. When covered by the waters, I am; and the ebb but reveals me again.

Sometimes it is the other way around. A white person is set down in our midst, but the contrast is just as sharp for me. For instance, when I sit in the drafty basement that is The New World Cabaret with a white person, my color comes. We enter chatting about any little nothing that we have in common and are seated by the jazz waiters. In the abrupt way that jazz orchestras have, this one plunges into a number. It loses no time in circumlocutions, but gets right down to business. It constricts the thorax and splits the heart with its tempo and narcotic harmonies. This orchestra grows rambunctious, rears on its hind legs and attacks the tonal veil with primitive fury, rending it, clawing it until it breaks through to the jungle beyond. I follow those heathen—follow them exultingly. I dance wildly inside myself; I yell within, I whoop; I shake my assegai[6] above my head, I hurl it true to the mark *yeeeeooww*! I am in the jungle and living in the jungle way. My face is painted red and yellow and my body is painted blue. My pulse is throbbing like a war

---

4. **Hegira:** flight of Muhammed from Mecca in A.D. 622; any journey, especially one undertaken to escape from a dangerous or undesirable situation.
5. **Barnard:** American women's college in New York City, near the Hudson River (cf. "by the waters of Zion").
6. **Assegai:** a light spear used by tribesmen in southern Africa.

drum. I want to slaughter something—give pain, give death to what, I do not know. But the piece ends. The men of the orchestra wipe their lips and rest their fingers. I creep back slowly to the veneer we call civilization with the last tone and find the white friend sitting motionless in his seat, smoking calmly.

"Good music they have here," he remarks, drumming the table with his fingertips.

Music. The great blobs of purple and red emotion have not touched him. He has only heard what I felt. He is far away and I see him but dimly across the ocean and the continent that have fallen between us. He is so pale with his whiteness then and I am *so* colored.

At certain times I have no race, I am *me*. When I set my hat at a certain angle and saunter down Seventh Avenue, Harlem City, feeling as snooty as the lions in front of the Forty-Second Street Library, for instance. So far as my feelings are concerned, Peggy Hopkins Joyce[7] on the Boule Mich with her gorgeous raiment, stately carriage, knees knocking together in a most aristocratic manner, has nothing on me. The cosmic Zora emerges. I belong to no race nor time. I am the eternal feminine with its string of beads.

I have no separate feeling about being an American citizen and colored. I am merely a fragment of the Great Soul that surges within the boundaries. My country, right or wrong.

Sometimes, I feel discriminated against, but it does not make me angry. It merely astonishes me. How *can* any deny themselves the pleasure of my company? It's beyond me.

But in the main, I feel like a brown bag of miscellany propped against a wall. Against a wall in company with other bags, white, red and yellow. Pour out the contents, and there is discovered a jumble of small things priceless and worthless. A first-water diamond, an empty spool, bits of broken glass, lengths of string, a key to a door long since crumbled away, a rusty knife-blade, old shoes saved for a road that never was and never will be, a nail bent under the weight of things too heavy for any nail, a dried flower or two still a little fragrant. In your hand is the brown bag. On the ground before you is the jumble it held—so much like the jumble in the bags, could they be emptied, that all might be dumped in a single heap and the bags refilled without altering the content of any greatly. A bit of colored glass more or less would not matter. Perhaps that is how the Great Stuffer of Bags filled them in the first place—who knows?

7. **Peggy Hopkins Joyce:** American beauty and fashion-setter of the twenties. "Boule Miche": the Boulevard Saint-Michel, a fashionable street in Paris.

GO ON

Responding to the Selection

Now that you have read the essay, respond to the following items as completely as possible.

1. Take a few minutes to write down your first response to the autobiographical essay.

_____

_____

_____

_____

_____

_____

_____

_____

_____

_____

_____

_____

_____

_____

_____

_____

_____

_____

_____

_____

_____

_____

GO ON

2. Think about a specific incident in the essay. In the box below, draw some of the images that this incident suggests to you.

On the lines below, explain why you chose these images and what they mean to you.

_____

_____

_____

_____

_____

_____

_____

_____

_____

_____

GO ON

3. After reading this essay by Zora Neale Hurston, imagine meeting the author at a party. What questions about the essay would you like to ask her? Explain why you would ask these questions.

_____

_____

_____

_____

_____

_____

_____

_____

_____

_____

4. Think of a person, real or fictional, who reminds you of the author of this essay. Describe the person and explain how he or she is like the author.

_____

_____

_____

_____

_____

_____

_____

_____

_____

_____

_____

| GO ON |

5. Imagine Zora Neale Hurston giving a speech at a high school graduation ceremony. What advice do you think she would give to the students about how to live their lives? What evidence in the selection makes you say so?

_____

_____

_____

_____

_____

_____

_____

_____

_____

_____

_____

_____

_____

_____

_____

_____

_____

_____

_____

_____

_____

_____

GO ON

6. Use this page to write down any additional thoughts you have about the autobiographical essay. Tell anything else about your understanding of the essay and what it means to you.

_____

_____

_____

_____

_____

_____

_____

_____

_____

_____

_____

_____

_____

_____

_____

_____

_____

_____

_____

_____

STOP!
DO NOT CONTINUE UNTIL INSTRUCTED
This is the end of the Reading Section

ASSESSMENT • 3

WRITING SECTION

Getting Ready to Write

You are going to write an essay for your English teacher that explains how the images in the final paragraph of Hurston's autobiographical essay describe her personal philosophy. Begin by examining some of the images Hurston uses in the concluding paragraph of her essay, and decide what those images tell you about Hurston's world-view. Use the chart below to list some of your ideas before you begin writing.

Images in the concluding paragraph:

Meanings of those images:

Hurston's philosophy:

GO ON

Sharing Your Plans With Others (Optional)

Before you begin writing, share your writing plans with some of your classmates. Using your notes, tell them about your interpretation of the concluding paragraph of Hurston's autobiographical essay. Ask your classmates questions like the following

- Have I selected appropriate images from the concluding paragraph?
- Have I interpreted those images in a meaningful and thoughtful way?
- Is my interpretation of Hurston's philosophy clear and supportable?

Jot down reactions from your classmates in the space below.

_____

_____

_____

_____

_____

_____

_____

_____

_____

_____

_____

_____

_____

_____

_____

You should also be prepared to give comments and suggestions about your classmates' writing plans. Try to give them honest and specific suggestions. Tell them about things they may want to delete or add. Suggest ways they can organize their ideas.

Thinking About Reactions

Spend a few minutes thinking about the comments and suggestions your classmates gave you. Review the notes you took when you met with them. Are there any changes you should make, based on their comments? Use the space below to write down any important ideas you received from your classmates or to revise your original writing plans.

_____

_____

_____

_____

_____

_____

_____

_____

_____

_____

_____

_____

_____

_____

_____

_____

_____

_____

_____

_____

_____

_____

_____

_____

GO ON

Time to Write

Write an essay for your English teacher that interprets the images Zora Neale Hurston uses in the final paragraph of "How It Feels to Be Colored Me." What is Hurston's philosophy, and how do these images convey it? Try to convince your readers that your interpretation is a thoughtful one by supporting your claims with evidence from Hurston's essay and from your own personal experience.

_____

_____

_____

_____

_____

_____

_____

_____

_____

_____

_____

_____

_____

_____

_____

_____

_____

_____

_____

_____

_____

_____

_____

_____

_____

_____

_____

_____

_____

_____

_____

_____

_____

_____

_____

_____

_____

_____

_____

_____

_____

_____

_____

_____

_____

_____

_____

_____

_____

_____

ASSESSMENT • 4

LEVEL F

NAME _____

CLASS _____

DATE _____

INTEGRATED
PERFORMANCE ASSESSMENT
STUDENT FORMS

ASSESSMENT • 4

READING SECTION

➤ Directions:

Today you will read an excerpt from an autobiographical essay. Then you will write about what you have read. You should write down your thoughts, questions, and opinions as you read. Your notes will help you when you write about the essay. When you finish reading, answer all of the questions about the essay until you come to the word STOP.

Getting Ready to Read

Hunger of Memory is an autobiographical essay by Richard Rodriguez, in which he examines his own emotional and intellectual development. In the excerpt included here, Rodriguez talks about his early formulas for success.

Time to Read

from *Hunger of Memory*
by
Richard Rodriguez

> My thoughts about
> what I am reading

In fourth grade I embarked upon a grandiose reading program. "Give me the names of important books," I would say to startled teachers. They soon found out that I had in mind "adult books." I ignored their suggestions of anything I suspected was written for children. (Not until I was in college, as a result, did I read *Huckleberry Finn* or *Alice's Adventures in Wonderland*.) Instead, I read *The Scarlet Letter* and Franklin's *Autobiography*. And whatever I read I read for extra credit. Each time I finished a book, I reported the achievement to a teacher and basked in the praise my effort earned. Despite my best efforts, however, there seemed to be more and more books I needed to read. At the library I would literally tremble as I came upon whole shelves of books I hadn't read. So I read and I read and I read: *Great Expectations*; all the short stories of Kipling; *The Babe Ruth Story*; the entire first volume of the *Encyclopaedia Britannica* (A–ANSTEY); the *Iliad*; *Moby Dick*; *Gone with the Wind*; *The Good Earth*; *Ramona*; *Forever Amber*; *The Lives of the Saints*; *Crime and Punishment*; *The Pearl*. . . . Librarians who initially frowned when I checked out the maximum ten books at a time started saving books they thought I might like. Teachers would say to the rest of the class, "I only wish the rest of you took reading as seriously as Richard obviously does."

But at home I would hear my mother wondering, "What do you see in your books?" (Was reading a hobby like her

GO ON

knitting? Was so much reading even healthy for a boy? Was it a sign of "brains"? Or was it just a convenient excuse for not helping around the house on Saturday mornings?) Always, "What do you see . . . ?"

What *did* I see in my books? I had the idea that they were crucial for my academic success, though I couldn't have said exactly how or why. In the sixth grade I simply concluded that what gave a book its value was some major idea or theme it contained. If that core essence could be mined and memorized, I would become learned like my teachers. I decided to record in a notebook the themes of the books that I read. After reading *Robinson Crusoe*, I wrote that its theme was "the value of learning to live by oneself." When I completed *Wuthering Heights*, I noted the danger of "letting emotions get out of control." Rereading these brief moralistic appraisals usually left me disheartened. I couldn't believe that they were really the source of reading's value. But for many more years, they constituted the only means I had of describing to myself the educational value of books.

In spite of my earnestness, I found reading a pleasurable activity. I came to enjoy the lonely good company of books. Early on weekday mornings, I'd read in my bed. I'd feel a mysterious comfort then, reading in the dawn quiet—the blue-gray silence interrupted by the occasional churning of the refrigerator motor a few rooms away or the more distant sounds of a city bus beginning its run. On weekends I'd go to the public library to read, surrounded by old men and women. Or, if the weather was fine, I would take my books to the park and read in the shade of a tree. A warm summer evening was my favorite reading time. Neighbors would leave for vacation and I would water their lawns. I would sit through the twilight on the front porches or in backyards, reading to the cool, whirling sounds of the sprinklers.

I also had favorite writers. But often those writers I enjoyed most I was least able to value. When I read William Saroyan's *The Human Comedy*, I was immediately pleased by the narrator's warmth and the charm of his story. But as quickly I became suspicious. A book so enjoyable to read couldn't be very "important." Another summer I determined to read all the novels of Dickens. Reading his fat novels, I loved the feeling I got—after the first hundred pages—of being at home in a fictional world where I knew the names of the characters and cared about what was going to happen to them. And it bothered me that I was forced away at the conclusion, when the fiction closed tight, like a fortune-teller's fist—the futures of all the major characters neatly resolved. I never knew how to take such feelings seriously, however. Nor did I suspect that these experiences could be part of a novel's meaning. Still, there were

From *Hunger of Memory* by Richard Rodriguez. Copyright © 1982 by Richard Rodriguez. Reprinted by permission of **David R. Godine, Publisher, Inc.**

GO ON

My thoughts about what I am reading

pleasures to sustain me after I'd finish my books. Carrying a volume back to the library, I would be pleased by its weight. I'd run my fingers along the edge of the pages and marvel at the breadth of my achievement. Around my room, growing stacks of paperback books reinforced my assurance.

I entered high school having read hundreds of books. My habit of reading made me a confident speaker and writer of English. Reading also enabled me to sense something of the shape, the major concerns, of Western thought. (I was able to say something about Dante and Descartes and Engels and James Baldwin[1] in my high school term papers.) In these various ways, books brought me academic success as I hoped that they would. But I was not a good reader. Merely bookish, I lacked a point of view when I read. Rather, I read in order to acquire a point of view. I vacuumed books for epigrams, scraps of information, ideas, themes—anything to fill the hollow within me and make me feel educated. When one of my teachers suggested to his drowsy tenth-grade English class that a person could not have a "complicated idea" until he had read at least two thousand books, I heard the remark without detecting either its irony or its very complicated truth. I merely determined to compile a list of all the books I had ever read. Harsh with myself, I included only once a title I might have read several times. (How, after all, could one read a book more than once?) And I included only those books over a hundred pages in length. (Could anything shorter be a book?)

There was yet another high school list I compiled. One day I came across a newspaper article about the retirement of an English professor at a nearby state college. The article was accompanied by a list of the "hundred most important books of Western Civilization." "More than anything else in my life," the professor told the reporter with finality, "these books have made me all that I am." That was the kind of remark I couldn't ignore. I clipped out the list and kept it for the several months it took me to read all the titles. Most books, of course, I barely understood. While reading Plato's *Republic*, for instance, I needed to keep looking at the book jacket comments to remind myself what the text was about. Nevertheless, with the special patience and superstition of a scholarship boy, I looked at every word of the text. And by the time I reached the last word, relieved, I convinced myself that I had read *The Republic*. In a ceremony of great pride, I solemnly crossed Plato off my list.

---

1. **Dante . . . Baldwin:** Dante Alighieri, Italian poet (1265–1321), author of *The Divine Comedy;* Rene Descartes, French philosopher and mathematician (1596–1650); Friedrich Engels, German writer and socialist leader (1820–1895); James Baldwin, American writer (1924–1987), author of fiction, essays, and plays.

From *Hunger of Memory* by Richard Rodriguez. Copyright © 1982 by Richard Rodriguez. Reprinted by permission of **David R. Godine, Publisher, Inc.**

GO ON

Responding to the Selection

Now that you have read the essay, respond to the following items as completely as possible.

1. Take a few minutes to write down your first response to the autobiographical essay.

_____

_____

_____

_____

_____

_____

_____

_____

_____

_____

_____

_____

_____

_____

_____

_____

_____

_____

_____

_____

_____

_____

_____

GO ON

2. In the chart below, make your own double-entry journal about Rodriguez's autobiographical essay. In the left-hand column, copy any passages (words, phrases, sentences) from the essay that seem especially important or interesting to you. In the right-hand column, write your thoughts about the passages you have selected.

PASSAGES FROM THE ESSAY	MY THOUGHTS ABOUT THE PASSAGES

GO ON

3. Rodriguez says that as a boy he determined that the educational value of the books he read was in the moral lesson or theme each book illustrated. Do you think that is a good reason for reading? Explain why or why not. In your opinion, what is the best reason for reading? Why?

_____

_____

_____

_____

_____

_____

_____

_____

_____

_____

_____

_____

_____

_____

_____

_____

_____

_____

_____

GO ON

4. Rodriguez said he read many books so that he would feel like an educated person. What do you think it means to be an educated person? In the space below, list characteristics of an educated person.

_____

_____

_____

_____

_____

_____

_____

_____

_____

_____

5. What do you think the author of this essay is trying to say about the value of reading?

_____

_____

_____

_____

_____

_____

_____

_____

_____

_____

_____

GO ON

6. Use this page to write down any additional thoughts you have about the autobiographical essay. Tell anything else about your understanding of the essay and what it means to you.

_____

_____

_____

_____

_____

_____

_____

_____

_____

_____

_____

_____

_____

_____

_____

_____

_____

_____

_____

_____

_____

_____

_____

STOP!
DO NOT CONTINUE UNTIL INSTRUCTED
This is the end of the Reading Section

ASSESSMENT • 4

WRITING SECTION

Getting Ready to Write

You are going to write an essay for your English teacher that evaluates Richard Rodriguez's childhood criteria for choosing books to read and compares those criteria with your own guidelines for choosing books to read. What criteria did Rodriguez have? What criteria do you have? How are they alike? How are they different? Use the chart below to list some of your ideas before you begin writing.

Rodriguez's childhood criteria for choosing books:
My criteria for choosing books:

Ways they are alike:	**Ways they are different:**

Support for my criteria:

Sharing Your Plans With Others (Optional)

Before you begin writing, share your writing plans with some of your classmates. Using your notes, tell them about your evaluation of Rodriguez's childhood criteria for choosing books. Ask your classmates questions like the following:

- Have I identified Rodriguez's childhood criteria for choosing books?
- Have I identified my criteria for choosing books?
- Have I thought of ways our criteria are alike and different?
- Can I support my criteria?

Jot down reactions from your classmates in the space below.

_____

_____

_____

_____

_____

_____

_____

_____

_____

_____

_____

_____

_____

_____

_____

_____

_____

You should also be prepared to give comments and suggestions about your classmates' writing plans. Try to give them honest and specific suggestions. Tell them about things they may want to delete or add. Suggest ways they can organize their ideas.

GO ON

Thinking About Reactions

Spend a few minutes thinking about the comments and suggestions your classmates gave you. Review the notes you took when you met with them. Are there any changes you should make, based on their comments? Use the space below to write down any important ideas you received from your classmates or to revise your original writing plans.

_____

_____

_____

_____

_____

_____

_____

_____

_____

_____

_____

_____

_____

_____

_____

_____

_____

_____

_____

_____

_____

GO ON

Time to Write

Write an essay for your English teacher that compares young Richard Rodriguez's criteria for choosing books with your own criteria. In order to determine what Rodriguez's guidelines for evaluating books were, you will need to refer back to his essay. Then compare your own criteria for evaluating a book to Richard Rodriguez's. If your criteria are similar to or the same as his, explain why they are good (or not so good) criteria. If your criteria are different, explain why they are better (or worse) than Rodriguez's criteria. Support your views with examples and details drawn from your experience.

_____

_____

_____

_____

_____

_____

_____

_____

_____

_____

_____

_____

_____

_____

_____

_____

_____

_____

_____

_____

NAME_____ CLASS _____ DATE _____

_____

_____

_____

_____

_____

_____

_____

_____

_____

_____

_____

_____

_____

_____

_____

_____

_____

_____

_____

_____

_____

_____

_____

_____

_____

_____

COPYING MASTERS OF CHECKLISTS

TEACHER _____   DATE _____

ASSESSMENT _____   CLASS _____

PART 1: OBSERVING THE READING PROCESS

SETTING OF THE OBSERVATION _____

USING EFFECTIVE STRATEGIES															
Sets own purpose for reading															
Makes connections between the text and prior knowledge and experience															
Anticipates and predicts what the author might say															
Thinks about words or phrases to stay focused on meaning															
Rereads if things don't make sense															
Seeks help from teacher or peers when necessary for understanding															
Takes marginal notes or draws diagrams to aid comprehension															

STUDENT NAMES

MARKING KEY	
+	Consistently
o	Occasionally
—	Never

TEACHER _____ DATE _____

ASSESSMENT _____ CLASS _____

PART 2: OBSERVING THE WRITING PROCESS

SETTING OF THE OBSERVATION _____

PLANNING																			
Uses prewriting strategies																			
Develops a plan before writing																			
Applies prewriting plans																			
Rewriting																			
Shows awareness of purpose and audience																			
Makes word-level revisions (e.g., spelling, punctuation, word changes																			
Makes higher-level revisions (e.g., adding ideas, removing parts, moving sentences or paragraphs)																			
Self-evaluating																			
Seeks reactions from others																			
Evaluates and uses the reactions of others																			
Reflects on quality of own work																			

STUDENT NAMES

MARKING KEY
+ Consistently
o Occasionally
— Never

Speaking/Listening Observational Checklist

TEACHER _____ DATE _____

ASSESSMENT _____ CLASS _____

SETTING OF THE OBSERVATION _____

STUDENT NAMES

SPEAKING

Volunteers for speaking activities															
Makes comments that are appropriate to the situation															
Expresses ideas clearly and accurately															
Presents ideas in an organized manner															
Supports point of view with logical evidence															
Responds logically to comments of others															
Rephrases or adjusts if others don't understand															

LISTENING

Attends to what others are saying															
Exhibits reactions (e.g., facial expressions) that reflect comprehension															
Understands directions without needing repetition															
Ignores distractions															

MARKING KEY

+	Consistently
O	Occasionally
—	Never

Model Papers with Annotations

ASSESSMENT • 1

READING: POEM
WRITING: OBSERVATIONAL ESSAY
(DESCRIPTIVE)

Responding to the Selection

Now that you have read the poem, respond to the following items as completely as possible.

1. Take a few minutes to write down your first response to the poem.

This woman has a very low opinion of her work
I can't tell if she even liked the poems that
she wrote, but she certainly didn't think
they were any good. She kept trying
to change them, to please other
people, but, in her opinion at least,
she only made them worse

response continues

2. In the box below, draw a picture of some of the images Bradstreet's poem brings to your mind.

On the lines below, explain the drawing or drawings you put in the box.

I put a mother and her child, because the poem relates the book metaphorically, to a child. I was hoping to somehow convey the mother trying to fix the daughter up, to make her better than she is, but I'm not that great of an artist. I also put a book, crossed out because it's a book that Bradstreet never wanted to see in print, that she would like to hide and forget about because it's not perfect.

response continues

3. Bradstreet uses an extended *analogy* to express her feelings about her book. An analogy compares two basically different things to show their similarities. In this poem, Bradstreet compares her book to a child. What does this analogy make you think about Bradstreet's attitude toward her book?

She sees it as a child who does not meet with her own approval. It's something she created, but does not like and would get rid of if she could. Knowing that this is not possible, she tries to make the best of things, but she can't change the book, just as one cannot change one's child. She gave birth to the book for herself, but suddenly the world is recognizing the child that she saw only as something ugly.

response continues

4. Think of another work (a song, story or novel, movie, TV show, or painting) that also deals with the theme of creativity. Describe the work and then tell how it is similar to or different from Bradstreet's poem.

Phantom of the Opera also deals w/ creativity in that the Phantom is writing this horrible creative, wierd opera. The difference is that he likes it while everyone else thinks it's trash. He wrote it for himself and will not allow it to be changed or altered in any way to conform to public opinion. Bradstreet does just the opposite, wishing to change her poems to make them look better.

5. Use this space to write down any additional thoughts you have about the poem. Tell anything else about your understanding of the poem and what it means to you.

I can sort of understand what Bradstreet is thinking. It's not that she hates her book, it's just that she never meant it to go farther than a hobby. She sort of feels like she's created a monster that has killed her little poems and made them into something that people can criticize and abuse. She would like to change them, to please everyone so that won't happen, but she can't.

Annotation for HIGH Reading Model • Score 6
This response reflects exemplary reading performance. The student understands the poet's use of figurative language, and accurately identifies it in the response to Item 2 ("... the poem relates the book metaphorically to a child"). The connection to *Phantom of the Opera* (Item 4) reveals reflective thinking about both works. The student's interpretation in the response to Item 1 (i.e., "This woman has a very low opinion of her work") might be questioned. However, in the response to Item 5, the student modifies the interpretation just enough to indicate a very insightful understanding of the ambiguity Bradstreet feels about her work ("It's not that she hates her book, it's just that she never meant it to go farther than a hobby").

Responding to the Selection

Now that you have read the poem, respond to the following items as completely as possible.

1. Take a few minutes to write down your first response to the poem.

This poem is hard to understand but small things can be picked out of it. It is well writen, in good format. I noticed parts about uglyness and unperfectness. It was a depressing poem. about her book.

response continues

2. In the box below, draw a picture of some of the images Bradstreet's poem brings to your mind.

On the lines below, explain the drawing or drawings you put in the box.

Drawing ① shows the casting
out from others, her book was
alone. ② identifies all of
her books deformities represented
by feet which arn't identical.
Number ③ represents her book with
clothes, how poor they were
and how poor her book was.

response continues

3. Bradstreet uses an extended *analogy* to express her feelings about her book. An analogy compares two basically different things to show their similarities. In this poem, Bradstreet compares her book to a child. What does this analogy make you think about Bradstreet's attitude toward her book?

She feels that her book is a cluster of thoughts all in one. Not everything makes scense or is in order. Everything came out when it wanted to and how it wanted to. Everything happened quickly and was done and over with before she knew it.

response continues

4. Think of another work (a song, story or novel, movie, TV show, or painting) that also
deals with the theme of creativity. Describe the work and then tell how it is similar to
or different from Bradstreet's poem.

> One of my own
> art works is similar. It
> is a painting of a wave
> all done in blue. The motions
> that I used tell a story
> of the wave. Everything
> the color, tecture and shading
> all just happened but support
> each other and the wave. It's
> not perfect.

5. Use this space to write down any additional thoughts you have about the poem. Tell
anything else about your understanding of the poem and what it means to you.

> It says that nothing
> is perfect. When one
> thing appears to get
> better another flaw is
> found. We can't look
> at these flaw- and be
> happy, we have to look
> at the greater thing
> and then we will enjoy life.

Annotation for MEDIUM Reading Model • Score 4
This student presents a generally thoughtful interpretation of the poem, although occasional
flaws are evident. In the last sentence of the otherwise weak response to Item 1, the student displays an important insight (the poem is "about her book"). The student's drawings in response
to Item 2 are symbolic and generally insightful, although it is unclear whether the student
understands that the word *feet* in the poem refers to poetic meter. The reponses to Items 4 and 5
are the paper's strongest features. They demonstrate the student's ability to connect with the
text on a personal and artistic level and to relate to the ambiguous feelings artists often have
about imperfections in their work.

Responding to the Selection

Now that you have read the poem, respond to the following items as completely as possible.

1. Take a few minutes to write down your first response to the poem.

The poem is about a mother who has a child who is slightly deformed. Rather than care for it, she tries to fix it and eventually ends up throwing it out of the house. My response to the poem is one of anger and sympathy. Anger towards the heartless mother who abandoned her child and sympathy towards the innocent child with no chance for survival now that his parents have basically disowned him.

response continues

2. In the box below, draw a picture of some of the images Bradstreet's poem brings to your mind.

A Landonment

On the lines below, explain the drawing or drawings you put in the box.

_____The drawing is of a person abandoning her_____
child. It reveals the evilness of the whole situation.

response continues

3. Bradstreet uses an extended *analogy* to express her feelings about her book. An analogy compares two basically different things to show their similarities. In this poem, Bradstreet compares her book to a child. What does this analogy make you think about Bradstreet's attitude toward her book?

Bradstreet doesn't like her book and feels it is slightly tainted. She likens it to a deformed child that nobody wants. She is saying that her book should be abandoned and nobody should ever claim it was hers.

response continues

4. Think of another work (a song, story or novel, movie, TV show, or painting) that also deals with the theme of creativity. Describe the work and then tell how it is similar to or different from Bradstreet's poem.

Another work that also deals with the theme of creativity is the T.V. show the smurfs. They are small and slightly deformed and abandoned. It is similar in the respect that the smurfs and the child are both different and can be considered outcasts.

5. Use this space to write down any additional thoughts you have about the poem. Tell anything else about your understanding of the poem and what it means to you.

The only misunderstanding I had in the poem was lines 5-7. They were unclear and difficult to understand. I just ignored the lines & moved on.

Annotation for LOW Reading Model • Score 2

In the responses to Items 1 and 2, this student demonstrates no ability to interpret the central metaphor of the poem. However, in the answer to Item 3, the student shifts to a more insightful understanding, perhaps due to the clues provided by the item itself. The reponse to Item 4 displays very limited success at making a meaningful connection to another work, and the reponse to Item 5 underscores the student's difficulty in interpreting the poem. Overall, this response merits a score of 2 rather than 1, based largely on the student's ability to somewhat refine his or her interpretation while responding to items about the poem.

Time to Write

You have a summer job working as an intern reporter at your local newspaper. Your editor has asked you to write an article about someone in your community who does something creative. You are free to write about anyone you choose. Your editor has told you that she wants an eyewitness account of what the person looks like while he or she is making or doing something creative. Be sure to use physically descriptive words and analogies to give your readers a good sense of what the person does and where she or he does it. Think of yourself as a camera, using words to take a picture.

Petite and plump, she sits confidently at her desk each morning. Her voice is both commanding and soothing, it is a voice of power and knowledge. She is my English III Honors teacher: Mrs. Campos. Mrs. Campos is among the many creative people I have encountered in life. Her creativity is not drawing in the field of art, her wobbly stick figures are proof of this. I have never heard her sing, or seen her dance, or do anything which publicly indicates a sense of creativity in her. Yet she is one of the most fascinating person I have ever known. Her creativity is in her knowledge, her voice. Mrs. Campos has a way of saying and expressing thoughts or just mere words. It is as if her voice was an invisible hand which probed into my mind and tested the consistency of my brain. She has a voice which soothes, commands, and demands at the same time; her voice is those of a comforting mother, a dictating leader, and a questioning child. For

response continues

Annotation for HIGH Writing Model • Rhetorical Effectiveness: Score 6

This response reflects exceptional achievement. The writer assumes an authoritative stance and conveys a strong sense of discovery while describing the subject (an English teacher) and, at the same time, analyzing the nature of creativity. The student skillfully weaves together observations of the subject with conclusions about creativity that do not fit the traditional mold (i.e., creativity limited only to musical or artistic talent). In addition, the writer clearly communicates the significance of the teacher's influence.

(annotation concludes on next page)

instance, ~ she said once, "No one outside of yourself can make you happy." My eyebrows rose as if in defiance ... my friends and close family relatives made me laugh, ~and~ smile, and feel good about myself. But, then, those same eyebrows lowered from thought ... yes, I could not smile or laugh unless I first felt good about myself. People who make me think, make me deny and accept ~~~~~~~ in the same breath fascinate me. Mrs. Campos is creative for that ~~this~~ incredible ability. Her creativeness cannot be seen, tasted, heard in melodious tones, or touched with ends of fingertips. Her creativity is much more complex and in-depth, her creativity makes a lasting impression in the mind.

Annotation for HIGH Writing Model • Conventions: Score 6
The response displays exceptional command of the conventions of written language. The response contains a few minor errors, but they are counterbalanced by its overall control.

Time to Write

You have a summer job working as an intern reporter at your local newspaper. Your editor has asked you to write an article about someone in your community who does something creative. You are free to write about anyone you choose. Your editor has told you that she wants an eyewitness account of what the person looks like while he or she is making or doing something creative. Be sure to use physically descriptive words and analogies to give your readers a good sense of what the person does and where she or he does it. Think of yourself as a camera, using words to take a picture.

Creativity has several different meanings, imagination, being yourself, exploring and art. There is one person who I would call creative and that would be Sue Chan (my mom) she is a ceramic teacher which means she teaches people how to make beautiful things. Sue Chan's ceramics and porcelin dolls are now on display in a popular magazine. Sue sculps her own dolls then makes their cloths and she still has time to have a job and keep a household together. People literally come from miles around to take one of her classes. Some of her classes are: eyelashes (for dolls) eyes skin tones, shading, sculpting, and these were only a few.

Sue Chan does not walk around in a white smok with paint and paint brushes in her hands. She wears her own style of clothing that

response continues

Annotation for MEDIUM Writing Model • Rhetorical Effectiveness: Score 4
This response reflects adequate evidence of achievement. The writer prefaces the observational essay by defining creativity and then introduces the subject of the observation (the writer's mother). The essay includes many details about the subject and her work. However, the biggest rhetorical weakness is the organization of the response. The physical description of the mother seems to interrupt the flow of ideas about her work. Nevertheless, the student has succeeded to a large extent in describing the subject, and the reponse receives a score of 4.

(annotation concludes on next page)

she wears to work and home. She has short hair, she is sort of short and has a real good sense of humor. Ave Chan teaches at her work Ceramics and Crafts and at Mary Beth's Ceramics. One is a warehouse full of paints, doll wigs, kilns, greenware and packaging the other place is a small shop with brushes, paints and greenware. And coming from her daughter, (me), I am always told how beautiful her dolls are and how they wish they could do what my mom does!

Annotation for MEDIUM Writing Model • Conventions: Score 4
The response displays reasonable use of the conventions of written language. The response is generally easy to read, but it contains errors in usage and mechanics that prevent it from meriting a higher score.

Time to Write

You have a summer job working as an intern reporter at your local newspaper. Your editor has asked you to write an article about someone in your community who does something creative. You are free to write about anyone you choose. Your editor has told you that she wants an eyewitness account of what the person looks like while he or she is making or doing something creative. Be sure to use physically descriptive words and analogies to give your readers a good sense of what the person does and where she or he does it. Think of yourself as a camera, using words to take a picture.

It was a Sunday afternoon when I notice my mother sitting at he sewing manchine making a dress for my sister for the play called Beauty and the Beast. I asked her what she was doing and she told me that she had to make a dress for my sister because the ones in the store was to expecive so she made the dress and when my mothr went to go get it dry cleaned I went with her and ask how come you did not just go out and buy one just like the one she made. She said "that it would cost me for the same dress over 500⁰⁰ but if I made it it would cost me on 55⁰⁰. So she made the dress and life went on.

Annotation for LOW Writing Model • Rhetorical Effectiveness: Score 2

This response reflects limited evidence of achievement. The student briefly describes her or his mother making a dress for a fraction of the price it would cost to buy one. The reader can infer that the mother is creative as well as thrifty. However, the writer has supplied no other details about the mother, the dress, or anything else that would make the paper an effective example of observational writing.

(annotation concludes on next page)

Annotation for LOW Writing Model • Conventions: Score 1
The response demonstrates great difficulty in applying the conventions of written language. There are numerous errors in usage, mechanics, and spelling. Among the errors that tend to interfere most with communication are several carelessly omitted word endings (e.g., "I notice[d] my mother sitting at he[r] sewing machine"; "it would cost me on[ly] 55^{00}").

ASSESSMENT • 2

READING: SHORT STORY
WRITING: PERSUASIVE ESSAY
(PERSUASIVE)

Responding to the Selection

Now that you have read the story, respond to the following items as completely as possible.

1. Take a few minutes to write down your first response to the story.

The "masque" — just as the title suggests — shows concealment, what things are supposed to be and what things are in reality. The masque had a very disturbing effect on me the reader. Where everything looks fine and the revelry persists, there exists an undertone of corruption, pestilence, and contagion unparalleled. Underneath the poor exterior there is evil.

2. If Prince Prospero were to tell you about his philosophy of life, what do you think he would say? What makes you think so?

Prince Prospero would deny the evil and even go so far as to revel in the glorious and prosperous conditions of within the castle. He would say "it is safe within my castle; no need to fear the dark of night. No evil may penetrate these walls where goodness prevails." Prince Prospero would tell his subjects and guests these things in order to keep their morale at a stable level. He doesn't want mutiny. He has to keep their trust. In order to do this he must tell them lies. He must wear a mask.

response continues

3. Read the following passage from the story and then write your opinions of the attitudes expressed in it.

> The courtiers, having entered, brought furnaces and massy hammers and welded the bolts. They resolved to leave means neither of ingress or egress to the sudden impulses of despair or of frenzy from within. The abbey was amply provisioned. With such precautions the courtiers might bid defiance to contagion. The external world could take care of itself. In the meantime it was folly to grieve, or to think.

The courtiers of the passage feel the need to keep the appearances of prosperity to fight their 'sudden impulses of despair or frenzy' from within. It is a human tendency, I think, to rationalize anything that goes wrong. In the situation of disease and death portrayed in "the Masque of Red Death" the courtiers symbolize denial, for they themselves must keep their own sanity in order to survive. "In the meantime it was folly to grieve, or to think."

response continues

4. Suppose you were planning to make a movie version of "The Masque of the Red Death." Thinking about other films you have seen that have powerful opening images, write a brief description of the first image you would have appear on the screen. Why would you choose that image?

The image I would choose to be presented as my opening scene would be of the huge black clock banging away in the dead of night, as described by Poe in his short story. To me the clock symbolizes the inevitability of death as time remains constant. Nothing can hinder it from moving on, or forces it to move backwards. It also shows that like time evil as a way of penetrating all things, such as in Joseph Conrad's Heart of Darkness, there exists in man dark truths to which cannot be denied. The tall, dark, clock's pendulum continues to its mechanical swing and provides the viewer with the uneasiness of imminent death.

response continues

5. Use this page to write down any additional thoughts you have about the story. Tell anything else about your understanding of the story and what it means to you.

The "Masque of Red Death" by Edgar Allan Poe represents a theme found in many examples of literature. That theme is of the truth that lies within, (whatever that truth may be) and how that truth is found. It depends on the individual and how that individual responds to it the use of "a thief in the night," Poe uses for symbolic purposes. If the individual is not ready, evil will come like a thief in the night and take over all.

Annotation for HIGH Reading Model • Score 6

This response reflects exemplary reading performance. The student insightfully interprets the significance of various elements in the story, such as the title (see Item 1). In the response to Item 2, the student's use of the word *prosperous* suggests an appreciation of the irony associated with the name "Prince Prospero." Unlike the score 4 Model Paper, this response goes beyond analyzing the character of the Prince and considers the more general theme of human mortality and "the inevitability of death" (see Item 4). Also in the response to Item 4, the student insightfully connects the theme of this story to another literary work (i.e., Joseph Conrad's "Heart of Darkness").

Responding to the Selection

Now that you have read the story, respond to the following items as completely as possible.

1. Take a few minutes to write down your first response to the story.

   Wondering about the significance of numbers and colors. Fate, destiny, just desserts?

2. If Prince Prospero were to tell you about his philosophy of life, what do you think he would say? What makes you think so?

   live life to the fullest, he who dies with the most toys wins. The Prince is so caught up in wealth and Fame he Believes he's immortal. he believes "Oh, look, all the pesants are dying, too bad. Maybe I'll have a party. Me and my friends will have fun despite this disease. We'll live in the lap of luxury with all my money and nothing will ever happen." Sort of a modern metaphor for AIDS. "It can't happen to me" even in Poe's time.

   response continues

3. Read the following passage from the story and then write your opinions of the attitudes expressed in it.

> The courtiers, having entered, brought furnaces and massy hammers and welded the bolts. They resolved to leave means neither of ingress or egress to the sudden impulses of despair or of frenzy from within. The abbey was amply provisioned. With such precautions the courtiers might bid defiance to contagion. The external world could take care of itself. In the meantime it was folly to grieve, or to think.

The Prince is a seclusionist. He thinks that every thing happening is sort of a let down. All he needs is his friends and his luxuory and every thing will be fine. There's nobody else he wants in, he is To selfish to let anyone Out. ~~But where~~ There should be no reason To leave any way. but who cares? Just have fun. The Peasants don't mean anything To us.

response continues

4. Suppose you were planning to make a movie version of "The Masque of the Red Death." Thinking about other films you have seen that have powerful opening images, write a brief description of the first image you would have appear on the screen. Why would you choose that image?

Open up with the face of a clock at 12:30. Start showing the Prince getting ready, greeting guests staring. Cutting in quickly with the shriek of a pesant at home newly aflicted. he continues, Theres dancing, laughter, then cut back to the peasants house again. More dancing, more singing, back to the peasant, blood streaming, in agony, The final guests arrive, the door is bolted shut, and in the echo of the "clank" of the door the peasant dies. Soft weeping from family members. Start heading up the road to The Palace. See coffin makers in Town, Quaranteen signs. Weeping families and finaly back to the Prince, who is sloshing down wine, making a mess of himself.

response continues

5. Use this page to write down any additional thoughts you have about the story. Tell anything else about your understanding of the story and what it means to you.

> Many Meanings can be aplied to This story. The most basic is man against death, then:
>   2) man against nature
>   3) man against Man
>   4) Fate vs. will

Annotation for MEDIUM Reading Model • Score 4

This response reflects thoughtful reading performance. The student understands the literal events of the story and also indicates an appreciation of some of the symbols in the story. He or she also presents a convincing interpretation of Prince Prospero's actions that connects the story with real life ("Sort of a modern metaphor for AIDS": Item 2). However, the response is not as insightful as score 5 and score 6 papers because the student focuses almost entirely on Prince Prospero's selfish attitude. Reflections or insights about more universal themes are hinted at but not developed in the response to Item 5.

Responding to the Selection

Now that you have read the story, respond to the following items as completely as possible.

1. Take a few minutes to write down your first response to the story.

I thought this story was weird + didn't understand it.

2. If Prince Prospero were to tell you about his philosophy of life, what do you think he would say? What makes you think so?

He would say that you can't isolate yourself from the rest of the world. He would say this because he tried to avoid the Red Death by secluding himself, but it still got him.

response continues

3. Read the following passage from the story and then write your opinions of the attitudes expressed in it.

> The courtiers, having entered, brought furnaces and massy hammers and welded the bolts. They resolved to leave means neither of ingress or egress to the sudden impulses of despair or of frenzy from within. The abbey was amply provisioned. With such precautions the courtiers might bid defiance to contagion. The external world could take care of itself. In the meantime it was folly to grieve, or to think.

They are acting as if they are better than the rest of the world. They think that nothing is going to happen to them if they isolate themselves from everyone and everything outside their walls.

response continues

4. Suppose you were planning to make a movie version of "The Masque of the Red Death." Thinking about other films you have seen that have powerful opening images, write a brief description of the first image you would have appear on the screen. Why would you choose that image?

I would show man, woman, and children, dying helplessly from these dissease. I chose these image because it portrays how deadly and powerful this dissease is.

response continues

5. Use this page to write down any additional thoughts you have about the story. Tell anything else about your understanding of the story and what it means to you.

I think this story is saying that it's alright to isolate yourself from the rest of the world, but don't ignore it and act like it's not there.

Annotation for LOW Reading Model • Score 2

This response reflects limited reading performance. The response to Item 1 is characteristic of a score 1 paper ("I thought this story was weird & didn't understand it"). However, in other responses the student displays some understanding of the story. The student seems to understand that Prince Prospero made an unsuccessful attempt to isolate himself from the plague, but responses are generally unelaborated, and there is little evidence of reflection about the deeper meaning of the story. The only response that attempts to state a general theme (Item 5) seems to contradict itself ("... it's alright to isolate yourself from the rest of the world, but don't ignore it and act like it's not there").

Time to Write

You have been asked to write a letter to the editor of your school newspaper. In your letter, you will take a position on a current controversy that affects people your age, and you will try to convince your readers that your position is reasonable. Your letter should define the issue, clearly state your opinion, present likely counterarguments and refute them, and give reasonable evidence that convinces readers to support your position.

Dear Editor,

Should HIV positive students be discriminated against in our nation's public schools?

Today, despite a growing awareness of the nature of the HIV virus and AIDS, there are still those who believe that those who have HIV or AIDS should not be allowed to attend public school with those who do not have either. I believe that our society needs to maintain a firm opposition against those who would deprive children of the basic right to an education on the basis of a prejudiced fear based on unsubstantiated notions.

People who believe this argue that these children will spread the disease to other innocent children. They argue that their own kids will catch HIV by playing and fighting with kids who are infected. They think the virus can be spread when children touch, sneeze, or cough on each other.

Scientists agree, however, that this is

response continues

Annotation for HIGH Writing Model • Rhetorical Effectiveness: Score 6

This response reflects exceptional achievement. The writer eloquently introduces the controversial issue, orients the reader, and assumes a very firm and authoritative stance. The student's treatment of counterarguments is not completely balanced and objective, but the writer supports the position taken with authoritative statements (e.g., "There is no evidence that it can be spread by a sneeze, a cough, or even a nosebleed as long as people take reasonable precautions").

(annotation concludes on next page)

highly unlikely. HIV is spread only when blood or internal body fluids are exchanged. It can spread when drug addicts share infected needles or when an infected person practices unsafe sex. There is no evidence that it can be spread by a sneeze, a cough, or even a nosebleed as long as people take reasonable precautions.

It is more likely that by removing HIV and AIDS infected kids from the public schools, and, thus, from society, the government would be supporting the irrational fears of the uninformed. They would allow society to become more afraid of those with the disease and cause a division in our society which would only give birth to hate, not help. Instead of supporting those who are infected, many would hate them for bringing the disease into the lives, and instead of helping them they would spurn them. Such an outragious act as removing these kids from school would not only be detrimental to the kids, but to our society as a whole.

Sincerely,
S. McPhee

Annotation for HIGH Writing Model • Conventions: Score 6
The response displays exceptional command of the conventions of written language. It is virtually error-free, with the only flaws being those typical of first-draft writing.

Time to Write

You have been asked to write a letter to the editor of your school newspaper. In your letter, you will take a position on a current controversy that affects people your age, and you will try to convince your readers that your position is reasonable. Your letter should define the issue, clearly state your opinion, present likely counterarguments and refute them, and give reasonable evidence that convinces readers to support your position.

Drugs are a major problem facing today's youth. Many people have asked the question "Should drugs be legalized?" Absolutely not. Drugs are dangerous and should stay out of our lives. A major argument for legalizing drug is that people need certain illegal drugs for medical reasons. An example would be smoking marijuana for eye problems or the ease physical pain. The truth is that drugs have negative long term effects that outweigh the short term positive effects. Besides, if a person seriously needs an illegal drug, there are legal ways of obtaining them. Another argument for legal drugs is that people might lose interest if it legal, because they enjoy the act of breaking the laws more than the drugs. However, legalization of drugs would only cause widespread addiction and increases in crime, I am afraid. Finally, the most outrageous argument is that Americans should be allowed freedom over their own actions. The bottom line is that drugs not only endanger an individual, but also endanger those around him or her. Drugs are an already huge problem to the youth and communities across America, legalizing them will only make

response continues

Annotation for MEDIUM Writing Model • Rhetorical Effectiveness: Score 4
This response reflects adequate achievement. The writer weaves the controversial issue question into the introduction and then presents a position and refutes possible counterarguments. However, the evidence is not presented in a particularly thoughtful or convincing way. For example, the first "counterargument" (that some people have legitimate medical reasons for using illegal drugs) could be easily refuted.

(annotation concludes on next page)

matters worse.

Annotation for MEDIUM Writing Model • Conventions: Score 4
The response displays reasonable use of the conventions of written language. A few usage and mechanics errors are evident, but the flaws are typical of first-draft writing and generally do not interfere with communication.

Time to Write

You have been asked to write a letter to the editor of your school newspaper. In your letter, you will take a position on a current controversy that affects people your age, and you will try to convince your readers that your position is reasonable. Your letter should define the issue, clearly state your opinion, present likely counterarguments and refute them, and give reasonable evidence that convinces readers to support your position.

Students should not have to pass standardized tests to pass. The tests do not reflect upon students grades and if a student cannot pass the test he or she will not be able to graduate. Standardized tests do show how a student compares to another student, but taking them is a waste of time. Students should be given a choice as to whether or not to take the test. Most will say they won't and the money spent for standardized tests will be reduced. Clearly the best move is for standardized tests to be eliminated.

Annotation for LOW Writing Model • Rhetorical Effectiveness: Score 2

This response reflects limited evidence of achievement. The student begins abruptly by mentioning a controversial issue without orienting the reader. Although a position against standardized tests is taken, it is not developed or supported. Also, no attempt to acknowledge and refute possible counterarguments is made.

Annotation for LOW Writing Model • Conventions: Score 3

The response receives a higher score of 3 for Conventions. Although usage and spelling are generally correct, several errors in mechanics are evident. In such a brief response, the errors prevent the paper from meriting a higher score.

ASSESSMENT • 3

READING: AUTOBIOGRAPHICAL ESSAY
WRITING: INTERPRETATION (EXPOSITORY)

Responding to the Selection

Now that you have read the essay, respond to the following items as completely as possible.

1. Take a few minutes to write down your first response to the autobiographical essay.

> The person in this essay has more sense then most people today, she was correct about everything she said. This person is exactly what every other person wants to be able to see themselves as.

response continues

2. Think about a specific incident in the essay. In the box below, draw some of the images that this incident suggests to you.

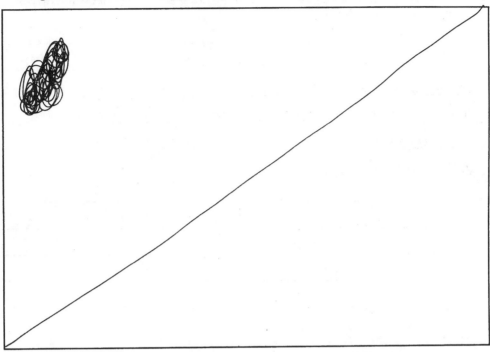

On the lines below, explain why you chose these images and what they mean to you.

The picture that is painted when they are in the basement listening to the Band. Suggests that Zora is very open minded and very spiritual She can allow herself to be taken away.

The section when she talks about the 3 bags filled with different things. These bags represent different cultures and suggest that it would not be so bad if the cultures were to mix a little without loosing site of the origin of each of the cultures.

response continues

3. After reading this essay by Zora Neale Hurston, imagine meeting the author at a party. What questions about the essay would you like to ask her? Explain why you would ask these questions.

I would ask her why she didn't care wither or not she fil in because it is harder to go against the grain, I would ask what motivated her to do her own thing.

4. Think of a person, real or fictional, who reminds you of the author of this essay. Describe the person and explain how he or she is like the author.

I can think of a real person who is similar to the Author because he dosn't worry about what other people are going to like he does what he likes and it just works out that everybody else likes it too.

response continues

5. Imagine Zora Neale Hurston giving a speech at a high school graduation ceremony. What advice do you think she would give to the students about how to live their lives? What evidence in the selection makes you say so?

First of all I do not belive that she would give any speech because that was not why she did anything but if she were I think she would tells everybody to do there own thing and not to become another robot of society.

response continues

6. Use this page to write down any additional thoughts you have about the autobiographical essay. Tell anything else about your understanding of the essay and what it means to you.

I feel that in order to truly understand the essay you really have to understand the time in which it took place. You must also think about why she does what she does.

Annotation for HIGH Reading Model • Score 5
This response reflects discerning reading performance. In the response to Item 2, the student critically evaluates the author's character ("Zora is very open minded and very spiritual"). The student is aware of the more obvious message concerning racial identity and comments on it in several responses (see Items 2 and 3), but the main strength of this response is the student's ability to see beyond the obvious theme of race relations and to appreciate the richness in the author's character and in her essay. The responses to Items 5 and 6 are adequate but not as insightful or as reflective as the responses to earlier items.

Responding to the Selection

Now that you have read the essay, respond to the following items as completely as possible.

1. Take a few minutes to write down your first response to the autobiographical essay.

The essay was a really trip. It's about segragation and how people responded upon her arrival to an all white school. I think they were wrong and just missing out on her friendship. She may be colored but she still thinks and acts like a human being.

response continues

2. Think about a specific incident in the essay. In the box below, draw some of the images that this incident suggests to you.

On the lines below, explain why you chose these images and what they mean to you.

The schools are very discriminet towards colored people. White people do not like something different (some.) They want every thing one way.

response continues

3. After reading this essay by Zora Neale Hurston, imagine meeting the author at a party. What questions about the essay would you like to ask her? Explain why you would ask these questions.

I would ask her how she felt when the white kids were prejudice towards her.

4. Think of a person, real or fictional, who reminds you of the author of this essay. Describe the person and explain how he or she is like the author.

Forest Gump. He was not the brightest person but some people didn't want to be around him and called him bad names (racisim).

response continues

5. Imagine Zora Neale Hurston giving a speech at a high school graduation ceremony. What advice do you think she would give to the students about how to live their lives? What evidence in the selection makes you say so?

Don't look at people from thier out side. You have to look past that and see whats really there. On the inside.

response continues

6. Use this page to write down any additional thoughts you have about the autobiographical essay. Tell anything else about your understanding of the essay and what it means to you.

Zora is right. We should all live under the same roof and look out for one another inestead of our great rivalry that we have today.

Annotation for MEDIUM Reading Model • Score 3

This student presents a plausible but basically literal interpretation of the essay. The student focuses on only one of many facets of the essay—the discrimination Zora Neale Hurston experienced as a student. The response misses the richness in the text and includes several predictable, almost trite, responses (e.g., Item 5). There are no major misconceptions evident, but the student does not provide enough reflection and insight for a higher score.

Responding to the Selection

Now that you have read the essay, respond to the following items as completely as possible.

1. Take a few minutes to write down your first response to the autobiographical essay.

My first response to this essay was that it was kind of dumb that one minute she knew her color and then the next minute she is saying she almost forgot what color she was because where she was. It was like one minute she was talking about her being a slave and her being black then she goes on to talk about Peggy Hopkins Joyce. Then she goes on to say that she forgot her name. The essay was real crazy to me. She doesn't explain clearly.

response continues

2. Think about a specific incident in the essay. In the box below, draw some of the images that this incident suggests to you.

On the lines below, explain why you chose these images and what they mean to you.

I chosed this image because talks about slavery and how she is the grandayghter of it. It just means to me that some white people still think that slavery is still going on today.

response continues

3. After reading this essay by Zora Neale Hurston, imagine meeting the author at a
party. What questions about the essay would you like to ask her? Explain why you
would ask these questions.

Why does she say her name
isn't Zora. when she goes other
places? What makes her keep
changing the subject about her
being black + that she dances
for money?

Because she doesn't give good
explanation for them.

4. Think of a person, real or fictional, who reminds you of the author of this essay.
Describe the person and explain how he or she is like the author.

Ruben Villa. Because he is
always changing the subject
doesn't give good explanation to
what he talks about.

response continues

5. Imagine Zora Neale Hurston giving a speech at a high school graduation ceremony. What advice do you think she would give to the students about how to live their lives? What evidence in the selection makes you say so?

I think she would talk about work hard at what you do and don't try to be like something you know you could ever be.

Because she talks about slavery, her not being known as Zora other places, not being colored some places she goes.

response continues

6. Use this page to write down any additional thoughts you have about the autobiographical essay. Tell anything else about your understanding of the essay and what
it means to you.

_I think she could have wrote
a better essay then this
because she just confused me
One minute she is Zora who is
black the next minute, she
really doesn't Know what color
she is._

Annotation for LOW Reading Model • Score 1
This response points out that lengthy answers do not necessarily reflect good comprehension.
In several responses (see Items 1, 4, and 6), this student expresses the kind of confusion and
frustration often found in low-scoring papers as he or she struggles unsuccessfully to make
sense of the text (e.g., ". . . it was kind of dumb that one minute she knew her color and then the
next minute she is saying she almost forgot what color she was . . .": Item 1). This student is
unable to follow the author's line of thought or to appreciate her playful use of language.

Time to Write

Write an essay for your English teacher that interprets the images Zora Neale Hurston uses in the final paragraph of "How It Feels to Be Colored Me." What is Hurston's philosophy, and how do these images convey it? Try to convince your readers that your interpretation is a thoughtful one by supporting your claims with evidence from Hurston's essay and from your own personal experience.

"How It Feels to Be Colored Me" is an essay which uses many symbols and analogies to make images and tell how the author sees the world, especially in the last paragraph.

I feel the last paragraph tells all about how she became the person she is. The brown bag she talks about stands for her and the things in it tell where she comes from. The other color bags are the variety that people come in. I feel the broken glass represents the broken dreams she had. The bent nail I feel stands for the weight of pressure she's been under. She says "a nail bent under the weight of things to heavy for any nail." Even though she has a upbeat attitude about her life I feel she has been under a lot of pressure. Like when she was the only black girl at school. The dry flower represents how she is weary but she still has some spirit left because she says the flower or two is still a

response continues

Annotation for HIGH Writing Model • Rhetorical Effectiveness: Score 5

This response reflects commendable achievement. In the first paragraph, the writer orients the reader and indicates that this response will focus on the "symbols and analogies" in the last paragraph of the essay. The student proceeds to identify and interpret several symbols (e.g., the broken glass, the bent nail, the dry flower). For each symbol, the student provides a plausible interpretation and supports some interpretations with evidence from the text. The response is not quite as insightful and compelling as a score 6 paper, but it is reflective and well organized enough for a score of 5.

(annotation concludes on next page)

little fragrant.

Finally the merging of the contents in the bags represents the hope that one day people will get along and respect each others differences.

I feel this is a story of hope. The analogies and symbols in the bag and her attitude in the essay make me think so.

Annotation for HIGH Writing Model • Conventions: Score 5
The response demonstrates successful use of the conventions of written language. A few minor errors characteristic of first-draft writing are evident, but none of the flaws interfere with communication.

Time to Write

Write an essay for your English teacher that interprets the images Zora Neale Hurston uses in the final paragraph of "How It Feels to Be Colored Me." What is Hurston's philosophy, and how do these images convey it? Try to convince your readers that your interpretation is a thoughtful one by supporting your claims with evidence from Hurston's essay and from your own personal experience.

> She feels like a brown bag of micilleNay proped against the wall w/other bags. They are all different iN color, but inside they all have basically the same contents, pieces of brokeN Glass, a rusty kNife, & aN old pair of shoes.
>
> She is saying that these bags are like people. Different colors oN the outside, but oN the iside, mostly the same. Full of brokeN dreams, lost hopes, & tools both used & unused for choices both takeN & left.
>
> Those are the thiNgs that make people who they are, Not the color of the skiN.

Annotation for MEDIUM Writing Model • Rhetorical Effectiveness: Score 3

This response reflects some evidence of achievement. The beginning of the essay is abrupt and shows a lack of sensitivity to the reader's need for orientation. The rest of the response attempts to summarize Hurston's philosophy, but the summary is brief and lacking in support and elaboration. The student makes no effort to convince the reader to accept her or his interpretation. Overall, the response merits a score of 3.

(annotation concludes on next page)

Annotation for MEDIUM Writing Model • Conventions: Score 3
The response demonstrates marginally successful use of the conventions of written language. Although it contains several errors in usage, mechanics, and spelling, it is not especially difficult to read and understand.

Time to Write

Write an essay for your English teacher that interprets the images Zora Neale Hurston uses in the final paragraph of "How It Feels to Be Colored Me." What is Hurston's philosophy, and how do these images convey it? Try to convince your readers that your interpretation is a thoughtful one by supporting your claims with evidence from Hurston's essay and from your own personal experience.

She goes to talk about she feels like a bag surrounded by all different colors she is trying to say that the world is feeled with alot of colors and she feels like a bag crumbled up in the middle of it. The images she feels is crazy like a broken glass with colors

Annotation for LOW Writing Model • Rhetorical Effectiveness: Score 1

This response reflects minimal achievement. It is confusing and difficult to read and describes only Hurston's feelings rather than her philosophy as it is reflected in the last paragraph of the essay. Even the description of the author's feelings is vague and unconvincing. Therefore, the response receives a score of 1.

Annotation for LOW Writing Model • Conventions: Score 1

The response demonstrates great difficulty in applying the conventions of written language. It is very brief yet contains numerous errors in usage, mechanics, and spelling. The errors make the response very difficult to read and interpret.

ASSESSMENT • 4

READING: AUTOBIOGRAPHICAL ESSAY, EXCERPT
WRITING: EVALUATION (PERSUASIVE)

Responding to the Selection

Now that you have read the essay, respond to the following items as completely as possible.

1. Take a few minutes to write down your first response to the autobiographical essay.

I view this description of Richard Rodriguez's childhood with both admiration and pity. The fact that Rodriguez possessed the desire and determination to learn impresses me imensly. (I don't believe that many people ever acheive such drive). However, it seems a shame that Rodriguez immersed himself in literature that was far advanced for his age. While the time spent poring over Dante and Plato was not necessarily harmful, it would have been much more beneficial for Rodriguez to have concentrated on works appropriate to his age and life experiences.

response continues

2. In the chart below, make your own double-entry journal about Rodriguez's autobiographical essay. In the left-hand column, copy any passages (words, phrases, sentences) from the essay that seem especially important or interesting to you. In the right-hand column, write your thoughts about the passages you have selected.

PASSAGES FROM THE ESSAY	MY THOUGHTS ABOUT THE PASSAGES
and by the time I had reached the last word, relieved, I convinced myself that I had read The Republic.	The irony is clear—reading is much more than word recognition; it involves comprehension, formation of opinions, and thought stimulation (None of which Rodriguez experienced)
I had the idea they were crucial for my academic success…	I personally don't believe that literature is crucial for academic (in terms of formal school education) success. Rodriguez could study the works yet draw little from them — one may successfully study literature long after they have graduated from school — maturity is the pivotal factor in understanding and gaining from literature

response continues

3. Rodriguez says that as a boy he determined that the educational value of the books he read was in the moral lesson or theme each book illustrated. Do you think that is a good reason for reading? Explain why or why not. In your opinion, what is the best reason for reading? Why?

I appreciate the fact that he recognized the importance of central themes or moral lessons. However, a book's value stems from the reader's opinions, examinations, and exploration of such themes. Memorizing a work's central idea involves little analysis. Literature becomes valuable when a reader challenges themselves to dissect such an idea and evaluate its truthfulness, practicality, and universality. Good literature incites deep thinking and the formation of a personal sense of morality.

response continues

4. Rodriguez said he read many books so that he would feel like an educated person. What do you think it means to be an educated person? In the space below, list characteristics of an educated person.

An educated person is
- aware of the past
- aware of the present
- aware of possible future consequences of past and present action
- able to analyze information
- able to reach conclusions based on observation and analysis.

5. What do you think the author of this essay is trying to say about the value of reading?

Reading is only as valuable as the maturity of the reader allows it to be. Reading's educational significance includes more than an entertaining story line or likeable characters. Rather, literature serves a positive purpose when the reader is able to analyze their own reaction to the work, thereby learning about themselves and their society. Reading is valuable when it results not in simple comprehension or memorization but in challenging thoughts and ideas.

response continues

6. Use this page to write down any additional thoughts you have about the autobiographical essay. Tell anything else about your understanding of the essay and what it means to you.

I enjoyed reading the passage because I was also an avid reader at a young age. As a junior in high school, however, I am able to look upon the literature I've read and evaluate its effect and significance. Authors such as Steinbeck and Plutarch are much more valuable when read at the age of 18 than when I was in 6th grade! I am fortunate to have taken advanced placement and honors english classes throughout high school. We read often and we read a great variety of works. However, regular english classes read far less. This is discouraging because I feel that these students aren't getting a chance to improve their ability to analyze great literature and appreciate such works.

Annotation for HIGH Reading Model • Score 6

This paper displays exemplary reading performance. Beginning with Item 1, this student offers alternative interpretations of the text ("I view this description of Richard Rodriguez's childhood with both admiration and pity") and goes on to develop and support them. The student is particularly skillful at offering alternative points of view while still respecting the author's viewpoint. Also, the student's critical interpretation of the author's ideas is sophisticated and mature. For example, this student points out that one of the purposes of reading is for readers to learn about themselves and society (see Item 5). Meaningful personal connections are evident in the response to Item 6.

Responding to the Selection

Now that you have read the essay, respond to the following items as completely as possible.

1. Take a few minutes to write down your first response to the autobiographical essay.

> I too am a lover of books. I would read all day long if my life wasn't so busy. I think, however, that Rodriguez was missing the point of reading. There are books with no educational merit, but instead provide a friendly diversion. Rodriguez would find these not worth while to read. He focuses on the numbers of books and 'themes'. He reads mass quantities of so-called 'learned' books, as if he would miraculously become educated. The purpose of reading is to involve yourself in character, to imagine what you would do with the given circumstances. You have to look deeper than just reading the word on the page, you must become the book. It helps formulate opinions and feelings — a philosophy. It is not the quantity of books on reads — but the quality in the way they read them.

response continues

2. In the chart below, make your own double-entry journal about Rodriguez's autobiographical essay. In the left-hand column, copy any passages (words, phrases, sentences) from the essay that seem especially important or interesting to you. In the
right-hand column, write your thoughts about the passages you have selected.

PASSAGES FROM THE ESSAY	MY THOUGHTS ABOUT THE PASSAGES
asked for names of important books, wouldn't read anything childish	childrens books are also valuable
mother asked what he saw	he didn't see, only read
read for theme	that's not the only point to reading
teacher – 2000 books } professor – 100 books }	missing concept of reading to learn – reading for pleasure.

response continues

3. Rodriguez says that as a boy he determined that the educational value of the books he read was in the moral lesson or theme each book illustrated. Do you think that is a good reason for reading? Explain why or why not. In your opinion, what is the best reason for reading? Why?

The theme of a book is a very integral part of the story, however, it should not be the sole purpose in reading a piece of literature. One must read for enjoyment - for the sheer pleasure of the written word. The theme, then takes on more meaning, as does symbolism, and writing style. The purpose of reading should be to immerse one yourself unto the woven plot, then to experience the feelings as the story progresses.

response continues

4. Rodriguez said he read many books so that he would feel like an educated person. What do you think it means to be an educated person? In the space below, list characteristics of an educated person.

1 has a philosophy based upon learned experiences

2 is open minded

has been through formal education

5. What do you think the author of this essay is trying to say about the value of reading?

The author of this essay is attempting to lead others not to read solely for educational merit, or theme, but for the larger picture.

response continues

6. Use this page to write down any additional thoughts you have about the autobiographical essay. Tell anything else about your understanding of the essay and what it means to you.

I realize that the author now realizes his shortcomings in reading only for theme. There is so much more to it than that. Reading opens new worlds, so much color even if the print is black on white paper.

Annotation for MEDIUM Reading Model • Score 4

This student displays a thoughtful interpretation of the essay. Beginning with Item 1, the student challenges the author's goal of quantity ("Rodriguez was missing the point of reading") and builds a case for quality of reading (". . . you must become the book. . . . It is not the quantity of books on reads—but the quality in the way they read them"). Some of the responses (see Items 2 and 4) lack elaboration, but there is enough evidence to suggest the student understands why Rodriguez is reflecting back on his childhood beliefs. When viewed holistically, the response merits a score of 4 in Reading.

Responding to the Selection

Now that you have read the essay, respond to the following items as completely as possible.

1. Take a few minutes to write down your first response to the autobiographical essay.

I dont think that reading all those books was healthy. He was reading just to say he read them not because he wanted to learn

response continues

2. In the chart below, make your own double-entry journal about Rodriguez's autobiographical essay. In the left-hand column, copy any passages (words, phrases, sentences) from the essay that seem especially important or interesting to you. In the right-hand column, write your thoughts about the passages you have selected.

PASSAGES FROM THE ESSAY	MY THOUGHTS ABOUT THE PASSAGES
#1 a book so enjable to read couldn't be very important	both phrases show that he is not reading for himself but for society, he reads to attempt to fit in in #1 and to gain praise #2
#2 what ever I read I read for extra credit	

response continues

3. Rodriguez says that as a boy he determined that the educational value of the books he read was in the moral lesson or theme each book illustrated. Do you think that is a good reason for reading? Explain why or why not. In your opinion, what is the best reason for reading? Why?

If you enjoy learning a moral then reading books with one strong lesson or theme is good for you. I on the other hand enjoy fiction. The best reason to read is to enjoy the book.

response continues

4. Rodriguez said he read many books so that he would feel like an educated person. What do you think it means to be an educated person? In the space below, list characteristics of an educated person.

know what they beleive
can express themselves logically
knowlegable of ideas different
than their own
open minded
interest in learning

5. What do you think the author of this essay is trying to say about the value of reading?

it differs from person to person,
the value of reading you
get is equal to the value
of your reason for reading

response continues

6. Use this page to write down any additional thoughts you have about the autobiographical essay. Tell anything else about your understanding of the essay and what it means to you.

It is upsetting to see him reading some many books and not getting anything. It is similar to how we read assigned books at school

Annotation for LOW Reading Model • Score 2
This response displays limited understanding of the essay. The student seems to focus on the single notion that Rodriguez read a lot of books but did not always understand them, rather than addressing the overall essay. The response to Item 4 is better than most score 2 papers, but other responses are very brief and literal (see Items 2, 3, and 6). When all responses are viewed holistically, this response receives a score of 2 in Reading.

Time to Write

Write an essay for your English teacher that compares young Richard Rodriguez's criteria for choosing books with your own criteria. In order to determine what Rodriguez's guidelines for evaluating books were, you will need to refer back to his essay. Then compare your own criteria for evaluating a book to Richard Rodriguez's. If your criteria are similar to or the same as his, explain why they are good (or not so good) criteria. If your criteria are different, explain why they are better (or worse) than Rodriguez's criteria. Support your views with examples and details drawn from your experience.

In the essay Richard Rodriguez chooses to read books that others find important, classics, often more advanced than he is ready for. He hopes that by doing this he will become as educated as his teachers. He read thinking that reading would "somehow further his academic success", but he didn't know just how reading would help him. By searching so hard for this information that would intellectually enlighten him, he missed many of the great gifts a book can present.

When I pick up a book first of all I do so because it is good entertainment. It is enjoyable to become absorbed in romances, daring adventures or simple stories about life. I read what I want to read. I couldn't read if I didn't find some enjoyment in it. I also read because it presents me with places, activities, and aspects of life that I am not involved with and know little

response continues

about. I helps me learn about the world and see things from different perspectives. Reading offers new ideas and encourages my imagination to work. Finally, reading provides me with insight of the minds of others, what they think and feel, and helps me learn about the human nature of people in general.

I feel that Richard's approach to reading is not helpful to him at all. By reading what others value, Richard tries to emulate the same effect that they got from the book. He analyzes the book searching for some message, he looses sight of the fact that reading is very personal and each individual gets something a little different from it. Richard also, allows his life to be swallowed up by reading and he misses much of the learning process that goes on simply by interacting with other people. I think that the reason he eventually finds comfort in reading is because he knows little about the "real" world, and being with "real" people and is afraid of going out into the world. It seems as though Richard will go on

response continues

Annotation for HIGH Writing Model • Rhetorical Effectiveness: Score 6
This student displays exceptional achievement in Rhetorical Effectiveness. Although the student does not offer an elaborate introduction to orient the reader, the paper is well organized and flows logically. The student presents Rodriguez's criteria as well as his or her own. Many of the evaluative judgments are orignal and fresh (e.g., "By reading what others value, Richard tries to emulate the same effect that they got from the book"), and most are well supported. The strength of this paper lies in the reasoning the student displays. The writer does digress into a discussion of the reading process and reading habits which detracts somewhat from the focus on *criteria* but manages to weave the discussion into the overall response.

(annotation concludes on next page)

reading books that he doesn't even understand, forever, because he is searching for something that isn't in books, it is inside him, his thoughts, his feelings.

In my opinion, my criteria for choosing books is better than Richard's. I allow reading to become personal so that I can get all of what the author is trying to say. I become absorbed in the book and actually live the experiences of the characters allowing myself to see the world from another point of view. I become emotionally involved and end up not only learning about other places and other minds, but about myself. I never forget to enjoy the reading and do not substitute books for the joys that living amongst others can bring.

I pity Richard, I think that if he were to die today he would have missed out on a lot of wonderful things. It would be as though he had never lived. Words, only say so much.

Annotation for HIGH Writing Model • Conventions: Score 5
This student demonstrates successful use of the conventions of written language. Although the paper is relatively error-free, it does contain some minor errors in usage and mechanics.

Time to Write

Write an essay for your English teacher that compares young Richard Rodriguez's criteria for choosing books with your own criteria. In order to determine what Rodriguez's guidelines for evaluating books were, you will need to refer back to his essay. Then compare your own criteria for evaluating a book to Richard Rodriguez's. If your criteria are similar to or the same as his, explain why they are good (or not so good) criteria. If your criteria are different, explain why they are better (or worse) than Rodriguez's criteria. Support your views with examples and details drawn from your experience.

In this excerpt from <u>Hunger of Memory</u>, Richard Rodriguez reveals his criteria for choosing books to read when he was a child. While most children read simplistic and enjoyable books at a young age, Richard Rodriguez was quite the opposite as he read long novels that were far beyond a child's reading level. Instead of reading for pure enjoyment, Rodriguez read to impress others and therefore in my opinion had a foolish criteria for choosing books as a child.

Rodriguez began reading long novels, always more than one-hundred pages, in the fourth grade. He ignored suggestions to read shorter and simpler books and arrogantly attempted to read far beyond his abilities Rodriguez missed out on the many great childrens books that his peers were reading at the time by reading long boring books such as <u>Crime and Punishment</u>. He went so far as to read a volume of the Encyclopedia solely to impress his teachers and librarians. Richard Rodriguez missed out on many of the joys of childhood because of the time he spent inside alone reading these lengthy books.

response continues

Annotation for MEDIUM Writing Model • Rhetorical Effectiveness: Score 4

This response represents adequate achievement. The student shows sensitivity to audience by introducing the subject in the first paragraph. The student also references specific information in the essay to support or illustrate a point. Perhaps the major weakness of this response is a lack of focus. The writer digresses into *describing* Rodriguez's reading habits rather than *evaluating* his criteria for selecting books. For example, the second paragraph is almost entirely description. Evaluative judgments tend to be somewhat superficial and not well supported. On balance, however, the paper merits a score of 4 in Rhetorical Effectiveness.

(annotation concludes on next page)

The subject matter of Rodriguez's books was also ridiculous for a child of his age. The abitruse books such as Plato's Republic and works by Dante and Descartes were extremely difficult for Rodriguez to understand. He admitted to having to read the book jacket of The Republic to remind himself what the text was about which proves that he was reading far beyond his comprehension level. A child of Rodriguezs age should be reading on a more simplified level and for enjoyment. There would be many opportunities in the future to read the difficult and higher level books when he could fully understand them.

The criteria that Richard Rodriguez followed for choosing books is far different than my personal criteria. While Rodriguez feels you should read difficult books to impress others, I feel that reading simple books for personal enjoyment is far more important. A child should develop an enjoyment of reading at a young age and save the more difficult books for the future. In my opinion, simple and enjoyable books are also important even if you don't impress others by reading them.

Annotation for MEDIUM Writing Model • Conventions: Score 5
This response merits a score of 5 in Conventions. The student displays successful, and at times skillful, use of the conventions of written language. The paper contains only a few minor flaws that do not interfere with communication.

Time to Write

Write an essay for your English teacher that compares young Richard Rodriguez's criteria for choosing books with your own criteria. In order to determine what Rodriguez's guidelines for evaluating books were, you will need to refer back to his essay. Then compare your own criteria for evaluating a book to Richard Rodriguez's. If your criteria are similar to or the same as his, explain why they are good (or not so good) criteria. If your criteria are different, explain why they are better (or worse) than Rodriguez's criteria. Support your views with examples and details drawn from your experience.

> In this essay Richard Rodriguez expressed his criteria for selecting books. My criteria are different however.
>
> Rodriguez's criteria include books that sound adult like books he knows to be important. No books which sound childish are included.
>
> My criteria on the other hand is simply books I think will interest me.
>
> I feel my criteria is better because will I get enjoyment and knowledge out of the books I choose he simply can say that he has read that book.

Annotation for LOW Writing Model • Rhetorical Effectiveness: Score 2

This student displays limited evidence of achievement. The response is organized logically into four paragraphs—introduction, Rodriguez's criteria, the student's criteria, and a comparison. Development, however, is extremely limited. The student basically lists ideas without expanding on them. The only evaluative judgment comes in the last paragraph where the student attempts to show why her or his criteria are better.

(annotation concludes on next page)

Annotation for LOW Writing Model • Conventions: Score 3
The response demonstrates marginally successful use of the conventions of written language. Errors in usage (e.g., subject-verb agreement) and mechanics are evident, and some of the errors disrupt the meaning of the response.

FIELD-TEST SITES

Alvord Unified School District
Riverside, California

Armona Union School District
Armona, California

Escondido Union School District
Escondido, California

Fowler Unified School District
Fowler, California

Fresno Unified School District
Fresno, California

Kings Canyon Unified School District
Reedley, California

Mattoon Community Unit #2
Mattoon, Illinois

Metropolitan School District of Decatur Township
Indianapolis, Indiana

Middletown Public Schools
Middletown, Connecticut

Mobile County Public Schools
Mobile, Alabama

Montgomery County Public Schools
Rockville, Maryland

Oakfield Alabama School District
Oakfield, New York

School District of Palm Beach County
West Palm Beach, Florida

School District #200
Wheaton, Illinois

Sweetwater Union High School District
Imperial Beach, California

Weber County School District
Ogden, Utah

Winslow Township Schools
Cedarbrook, New Jersey